The
COPING
Strategy

The
COPING
Strategy

Choosing a Life of Wholeness in a Broken World

Larry R. Gillespie

BROWN BOOKS
PUBLISHING GROUP

The COPING Strategy
Choosing a Life of Wholeness in a Broken World

Brown Books Publishing Group
16250 Knoll Trail Drive, Suite 205
Dallas, Texas 75248
www.BrownBooks.com
(972) 381-0009

A New Era in Publishing™

ISBN 978-1-61254-245-4
LCCN 2015934615

Printed in the United States
10 9 8 7 6 5 4 3 2 1

For more information or to contact the author, please go to www.CopingStrategyInternational.com

*To "Baby," my beloved wife, who has been my
number one cheerleader during this book's
completion, and to the memory of Ruby, Buck,
and Bert, gifts from God, whose lives taught me
many of my greatest lessons about wholeness.*

Contents

Author's Note

What if it were possible for you to live in a much happier and significantly more fulfilled manner? What if there really were universal principles that could be practically applied, guaranteed to empower you to rise above the inevitable challenges of everyday life? What if these principles ultimately revealed the way to a life of personal wholeness? The COPING Strategy has been successfully employed to accomplish these objectives.

But this message comes crashing into a world of ubiquitous brokenness. Broken governments, broken economies, broken industries, broken communities, broken schools, broken churches, broken families, broken relationships, broken promises, broken dreams, and broken hearts—these are matters that so often consume our energy and ultimately seize our days.

Now imagine yourself living a life of joy and fulfillment, embracing principles guaranteed to empower you to rise above inevitable everyday challenges. Envision sharing these newly found tools for living and personal wholeness with family, friends, and coworkers. You choose to be there, and the COPING Strategy will guide you as you embark on this fascinating journey.

The COPING Strategy evolved over several decades as I presented it in various settings to hundreds of children and adults. Its principles have been shared with students, parents, teachers, school bus drivers, school administrators, secretaries, counselors, social workers, nurses, physicians, psychologists, single adults, senior adults, military personnel, church leaders, and many others.

The truths embedded within this strategy are universal, reflected in the literature of research-based psychology and anchored in the wisdom of the sacred writings. However, when I began my university studies in psychology a number of years ago, I was a bit of an enigma to some of my Christian friends. From their perspective, much of Judeo-Christian theology and the discipline of psychology were mutually exclusive and irreconcilable. But through the study of the Holy Scriptures, I have gained my greatest insight into the dynamics of human behavior. Indeed, these sacred writings have become my primary psychology text. They provide a standard by which I measure all theory and principle.

In creating the COPING Strategy, I have collected the wisdom of ancient philosophy and the world's acclaimed thinkers and research scientists, alongside the truths of the sacred writings. On the pages that follow, I simply provide a ribbon that ties them all together. These are the principles that will help you create a more joyful, healthy, and fulfilled life ever after. These are the truths that build a life of wholeness in the midst of a broken world.

Chapter 1

"WOW! I'M STRESSED OUT!"

"These things I have spoken unto you,
that in me ye might have peace. In the world ye
shall have tribulation: but be of good cheer;
I have overcome the world." (John 16:33)

The words of Jesus Christ reflect His divine wisdom and insight and tell us tribulation or stress is an inevitable part of the human condition. Yet He assures us we are not destined to become hopeless victims. There is provision for us to experience an inner peace that transcends human understanding.

You and I deal with stress on a daily basis. Sometimes, we're so deep into it, we don't even recognize the crazy things we do trying to overcome it. We're like the aspiring young man working in New York City's high-pressure financial district, who left his office promptly at five o'clock each evening to catch the Staten Island ferry and make it home in time for dinner with his family. One evening, running late, he got to the dock and found the boat out a few feet from

1

shore. He broke into a mad dash, followed by a daring leap that left him clinging with one hand to his briefcase and the other to the rail of the boat.

After pulling himself on board and dusting off the seat of his trousers, he exclaimed, "Wow! I'm stressed out!"

"Apparently so, son," said an elderly woman who had been watching the whole scenario. "This boat is coming in!"

Do you identify with this story? Have there been times in your life when the harder you tried to get ahead, the more behind you got? My guess is, if you are alive and breathing, the answer is yes.

In our pressurized world, stress is everywhere. We read about it in the morning headlines, and we experience it in our personal lives. Sometimes, like the young businessman, we get burned out. Though many of us struggle with the strain of everyday living, few people have resources that prove to be most helpful.

Decades ago, Alvin Toffler coined the term *future shock*, referring to the shattering stress we experience when we are subjected to too much change too rapidly. A single day in our lives can establish a line of demarcation between what came before and what will always be experienced as after. These are days that change our lives forever—the bombing of Pearl Harbor, the assassination of President Kennedy, the explosion of the *Challenger*, and the infamous events on September 11, 2001, which shattered the myth to which many of us had clung, that terrorism would always occur somewhere else.

Such days are not always so global in their impact. They can be as personal as a difficult family move, the ending of a valued relationship, the death of a loved one, a significant financial loss, the loss of a cherished ideal, the diagnosis of a dreaded disease, or a horrible accident.

Births, baptisms, and marriages also change our lives forever. Though these are usually embraced as happy occasions, they are often accompanied by a considerable degree of stress. Alongside the most distressful occasions, these events are indelibly posted in bold print on the timelines of our lives. How well we weather the challenges of these days will largely depend upon the coping skills we have developed.

A Transformational Choice

Choosing to develop constructive coping skills is the first step in transforming your life. It certainly changed the life of one of my dearest friends. Like the rest of us, Freddie has made many constructive choices in life, but he has also made some undesirable ones that caused a lot of pain. However, years ago he turned a new page, rededicated himself to God, and became an avid student of the scriptures. He not only read his Bible but also lived the scriptures. As he applied scriptural principles to his life, he evolved into a new man. No doubt, much of this metamorphosis was a result of the fervent prayers of his loving and faith-filled mother.

Freddie followed his mother's lead and began to ask God for favor and blessing. He asked God for forgiveness and for a wife who would be of His will. Trusting that God knew his desire and loved him unconditionally, Freddie waited for the answer to his prayers and took initiative.

On a missionary trip to South America, he met Josie, a beautiful Christian lady inside and out. They had a storybook courtship and a wonderful marriage. Then one day, the unimaginable happened. Josie, still in her thirties and full of God's love, was diagnosed with cancer. The disease quickly ravaged her body.

I witnessed Freddie's grief in the days and months following Josie's death. He grieved as deeply as he had loved. The emotions he experienced were normal, but the critical matter was how he would choose to respond to those emotions. What choices would he make? Would they be helpful, or would they compound his grief? Would he use the pain to make himself better, or would he choose the role of a victim and become bitter?

Freddie's grief work was not an easy process, but he applied the principles outlined in the COPING Strategy. As he capitalized upon his physical, emotional, and spiritual resources, he began a journey to recovery.

His journey had really begun years earlier, when he turned that new page in his life. At that time, Freddie made a paradigm shift in his perception and response to the world around him. He chose to live his life from the inside out rather than from the outside in, and this helped him avoid becoming a victim of his grief. He chose to see himself as God sees him—a loveable and capable child of God who overcomes through the power and grace that have been given to him.

During the days that followed Josie's death, one thing became clear: Freddie had not lost his faith. He loved God, and he was certain that He could bring meaning and purpose out of his great loss. He talked to God, meditated upon the scriptures, and came to know in his spirit that God remained mindful of him.

As the Holy Scriptures prescribed in 2 Corinthians 10:5, Freddie took thoughts "into captivity," processing his grief and refusing to become trapped in the destructiveness of negativity. As he prayed, he waited to find out what God had in store. In due time, he chose to exercise initiative and move forward.

Freddie also learned the healing power of giving. He graciously accepted favor from others when it was the responsible thing to do, and he was no stranger to giving to others in the same way.

Like every one of us, Freddie is less than perfect, but he knows what being redeemed means. Freddie is one of my heroes. In his imperfect life, the principles of the COPING Strategy have paid untold dividends. Putting these principles into practice has vastly contributed to his quality of life and to the lives of those around him.

The Nature of Stress

Grief like Freddie's can bring about a level of stress that can do real damage to body, soul, and spirit if it is not managed effectively. Stress triggers the body's fight-or-flight mechanism, which is designed to be both immediate and efficient. When we are confronted with a stressor, real or imagined, the body responds automatically by attempting either to fight the danger or to flee from it.

Unlike our more primitive ancestors, many of us are much less likely to be confronted with situations that present immediate physical danger, such as wild animals, warring neighbors, or harsh physical environments. Much of the stress we encounter is related to financial problems, difficulties in the workplace, family conflicts, and spiritual crises.

What's more, we seldom literally engage in fight-or-flight behavior. Rather than acting out or running away, our cultural training inclines us to restrain ourselves in such situations. As a result, unless we have an effective management strategy, we become victims to the harmful effects of stress.

In acute stress, the responding chemicals and hormones coursing through our bodies dissipate quickly, and any harmful effects are minimal. The problems emerge with chronic stress when the stress response is switched on and stays on. In this state, our bodies remain bathed in substances that become destructive in the long-term.

The choices we make in response to stress can sometimes result in destructive behaviors—overeating, smoking, alcohol and drug abuse, inappropriate or abusive relationships, slothfulness, and countless other negative lifestyles. Indeed, as modern medical advances have added to the average life expectancy, a self-destructive lifestyle has emerged as a primary cause of premature death. *The Doctors' Guide to Instant Stress Relief* suggests creating a "life style" instead of a "death style"—one choice at a time.

A Message of Hope

Learning, practicing, and embracing the six choices in the COPING Strategy yields the freedom and opportunity to embrace a life style over a death style. By managing your stress effectively, you create a more joyful, healthier, and fulfilled life.

The COPING Strategy does not involve specialized training or complicated long-term therapy. The six steps of the strategy are easy to learn and powerful in their ability to promote big changes in your life. As you apply it, you will

7

begin to feel empowered to transcend stress, depression, hopelessness, alienation, and anxiety through constructive thought, choice, and action. In time, you will replace the negative with the positive and experience an abundance of joy.

In my own life, I have had many opportunities to practice these coping skills. I count them as valuable learning experiences. Each challenge offered its pearl of wisdom, often in a form I least expected. One of the darkest times was a Saturday in December 1988. We were well into the holiday season. Our traditional Christmas party was scheduled for that evening. This festive event had become my family's way of expressing generosity to our friends in gratitude for the gift of their friendship. Together we celebrated the coming of God into our world. It was always a wonderful, happy time.

But that year, the party never happened. That morning, in a matter of moments, everything changed.

Poppa awakened me before dawn. "Something is wrong with Momma," he said.

I rushed to her bedside. She was unresponsive. A quick call to 911 brought the ambulance.

Pacing the floor at Baptist Medical Center, I felt the depth of my love for Momma. You see, when I was born in a little town in the heart of the West Virginia coalfields, my mother couldn't keep me. But her sister, Ruby, and Ruby's husband, Buck, were there when I needed them. They took me home. Ruby and Buck became Momma and Poppa, and we loved each other deeply. It was a love that bore the fingerprints of God.

The attending physician in the emergency room informed me that Momma had suffered a massive stroke. Though she was unconscious, he told us, she remained very much alive. "Hold on to hope," he said.

I tried to be hopeful, but the physician who had treated her high blood pressure for years had warned me there would be an episode like this. "It will not be forgiving," he said.

As I waited for news, my thoughts raced, and I became increasingly anxious. My body ached in places I didn't even know were there. My spirit felt drained of life's meaning and purpose. It was one of the most stressful times of my life.

And then, something unusual happened.

A mysterious woman appeared from behind a curtain, approached me quietly, and placed a note in my hand.

"Hang in there," it said. "Remember: There is no decision you have to make that God doesn't feel you can handle. Peace to you." She signed it, "Linda."

Her gesture and those few simple words embodied the principles of the COPING Strategy—the power of Choice, the power of Self-efficacy, the power of Faith, the power of Initiation, the power of Thought, and the healing power of

Giving, which naturally flows from the empathy of a loving heart.

Linda placed this note in my hand three days before Momma died. She disappeared as quickly as she appeared, but her fleeting presence in my life and her note, carrying its powerful, energizing message, continue to resonate within me and countless others with whom their impact has been shared.

You will be amazed at how Linda and her note have made subsequent appearances in my life. We will talk more about that later. For now, let us turn our attention to the power that choice has upon our lives and more specifically to the COPING Strategy with its power to transform.

THE COPING STRATEGY
A Plan of Choice

CHOOSE TO **C**OMPENSATE CONSTRUCTIVELY: I will choose to exercise my free will in order to make decisions that will foster the development of my growth and the growth of those with whom I am involved. I will choose to acknowledge those factors in my life that I can control and those I cannot control. I will choose to recognize that although there are many factors in my life over which I have little or no control, I do have control over how I decide to respond to those factors. I will choose to live my life from the inside out rather than from the outside in; therefore, I will not be victimized. I will choose to accept responsibility for my own behavior. I will choose to evaluate my behavior asking: 1. "What am I doing?" (Awareness) 2. "Is it helping?" (Assessment) 3. If it is not helping, I will ask: "What can I do that will help?" (Alternatives) <u>**BOTTOM LINE**</u>: I will choose to do that which is right.

CHOOSE TO **O**VERCOME: Each day I will choose to recognize that I am an overcomer. I will choose to perceive myself as being lovable and capable. I will choose to capitalize on my strengths in order to compensate constructively for my weaknesses. <u>**BOTTOM LINE**</u>: I will choose to be successful.

CHOOSE TO **P**AUSE TO NURTURE YOUR SPIRIT: I will choose to set aside a specific time for privacy each day to pause in order to nurture my spirit. I will choose to find meaning and purpose in my life. <u>**BOTTOM LINE**</u>: I will choose to take care of my inner self.

CHOOSE TO **I**NITIATE: I will choose to utilize the resources available to me in order to initiate specific strategies that will help. When I choose not to act, I will do so because it is the constructive thing to do, rather than a result of my irresponsibility. <u>**BOTTOM LINE**</u>: I will choose to begin when it is time to act.

CHOOSE TO **N**EGATE NEGATIVE THINKING: I will choose to do a checkup from the neck up each day. I will choose to acknowledge the power of my thoughts and will decide to be positive. I will choose to recognize that I am not disturbed by people, things, and events, but rather the views that I decide to have of them. <u>**BOTTOM LINE**</u>: I will choose to emphasize the positive.

CHOOSE TO **G**IVE: Each day I will choose to recognize the healing power of giving. I will choose to give to others and also allow them to give to me in a manner that is constructive. <u>**BOTTOM LINE**</u>: I will choose to help others and will allow others to help me.

Chapter 2

CHOOSE TO COMPENSATE
CONSTRUCTIVELY

"[C]hoose you this day whom ye will serve . . .
we will serve the LORD." (Josh. 24:15)

The first step in the COPING Strategy sets the stage
for creating your whole life in the midst of a broken
world. Each step is prefaced by the one word that is key to
successfully transforming your life: "Choose."

In my work, I have often counseled those who struggle
with the effects of overwhelming stress. Armed with degrees
in counseling and psychology, I draw on the teachings of
the world's great scholars, as well as on the scriptures and
particularly the words of the Master Teacher, Jesus Christ.
Alongside these marvelous resources, I have the children
with whom I have had the pleasure to interact at the numerous schools I have served as a school psychologist across
many years. They have taught me valuable lessons that I pass
on in the COPING Strategy.

I remember one group of high school boys quite well.
They were referred to me because they were acting out in

school. Introducing the COPING Strategy during our first session, I presented them with a very complicated maze.

One young man studied it intensely and exclaimed, "Wow! Lots of choices."

"Yeah, and the ones you choose determine the outcome," another student said.

All my years of formal education could not have enabled me to introduce the concept of constructive decision making more simply and effectively.

Like a complex maze, life is full of challenges and choices. The late Og Mandino, in one of his inspirational books, *The Choice*, says that many among us remain locked in perpetual states of failure and discontent because we do not recognize that we have a choice.

The truth of the matter is that there are things you and I can do in the worst of situations that can make a big difference. Think of the musical composition of a minor chord, the notes resonating a dark, melancholy mood. By simply raising the third of the chord by a half step, the musical landscape is transformed into a lighter and brighter tone. So it is as we play upon the strings we have been given in life. Even the smallest rearrangement can have the most dramatic effect. It is simply a matter of choice.

The COPING Strategy is all about learning to choose what will best resonate upon the soundboard that we call life. The primary takeaway of this book is the realization that while there are many factors in life that we do not have control over, God has given us control over how we choose to respond to them. Can you think of a better way to spell empowerment?

The Power of Choice

The power of choice lies at the heart of the COPING Strategy. That power is called free will, and, once we acknowledge it, we seize a certain amount of control over our lives. Free will does not mean we have control over everything that happens to us. We do not have control over many situations, but we do have control over how we choose to respond to those situations. This empowering acknowledgment allows us to live our lives from the inside out rather than from the outside in.

The impact of choice and sense of personal control can be a matter of life and death, as illustrated by a study involving two sets of nursing home residents. Researchers afforded first-floor residents extra choice and control in their lives, letting them choose what they wanted for breakfast, sign up for movies in advance, pick the night they wanted to attend, and select an indoor plant to place in their rooms, which they were invited to care for. The second-floor residents had fewer choices, but they had all kinds of wonderful things done for them. They were told what they would have for breakfast and when. They had no say in their movie night schedules, and, though plants were made available for them as well, they were instructed that a nurse would select one and take care of it.

When the researchers returned to the nursing home eighteen months later, the members of the first-floor group, which had been given choice and control, were more active and happier, and fewer of them had died. The results of the study illustrate the phenomenal power of choice and the critical importance of a sense of personal control.

Wars are fought over power on the battlefield, and battles are waged in the living room. Confront a two-year-old with the word "No!" or try to seize control of the remote during Monday night football and get ready for a power play. *Empowerment* has been a buzzword for longer than many of us can remember.

This sense that we have power over our lives is given to us through God. Jesus Christ said, "All power is given unto me in heaven and earth" (Matt. 28:18), and Saint Paul later said, "But we have this treasure in earthen vessels, that the excellency of the power may be of God, and not of us" (2 Cor. 4:7). In other words, when we, the earthen vessels, make constructive choices, the very power of God resides within us.

When power is exercised constructively, it is an essentially healthy aspect of our human development and functioning. Unfortunately, those who are overwhelmed by mismanaged stress often share a feeling of powerlessness and the perception that there are no choices that can make a constructive difference.

Taking Responsibility

"God grant me the serenity to accept the things I cannot change, the courage to change the things I can, and the wisdom to know the difference." — Reinhold Niebuhr

Control can be a good thing unless we are trying to control something over which we have no control. In addition, control must be accompanied by a sense of personal responsibility. Years ago, I came across an anonymous remake of the Serenity Prayer, which drives this thought home: "God grant me the serenity to accept the people I cannot change, the courage to change the one I can, and the wisdom to know it's me."

Taking responsibility is central to a healthy sense of empowerment, but it does not come as second nature to everyone. The classroom is a perfect place to observe the difference between those who see themselves in control and those who see themselves as victims. Some students see their grades as the results of their personal abilities and efforts: "If I had studied longer instead of playing that computer game, I could have aced that test." Others think their grades are the result of chance or a poor instructor who grades unfairly:

"If the teacher would explain it better, I would get better grades."

If you believe the choices you make have a significant impact upon your destiny, you have what is referred to in scientific terms as an *internal locus of control*. If factors such as luck and fate control your choices, you are said to have an *external locus of control*. Externals are less likely to believe that their efforts will lead to success. Consequently, they are also less likely to be motivated to achieve.

Externals can lead healthy and productive lives, and internals can be unhealthy and unstable, but research indicates individuals with a more internal locus of control tend to be more *stress hardy*. They generally have a more positive outlook, experience less distress, are physically healthier thanks to less chronic stress, and report more contentment with their lives. On the other hand, externals are more vulnerable to the negative aspects of stress. They are more prone to depression as a result of feeling they have no control over their fates. Developing an awareness of our locus of control can help us make the shift from being primarily external to internal, if needed, and begin experiencing a sense of responsibility for our successes along with our missteps.

Learned Helplessness

Many people are not unlike circus elephants, chained to iron stakes from a very young age to prevent them from escaping. In *The 4:8 Principle*, Tommy Newberry describes what happens to the young elephants after they grow up: Even after they have grown into massive, powerful creatures, they remain easily controlled using the same small stakes. Although they are perfectly capable of jerking the stakes out of the ground and escaping, they do not. They don't even try.

The elephants exhibit what is called *learned helplessness*. Prior experience teaches them to behave helplessly even when they have an opportunity to help themselves. Just like the elephants, many people live without any awareness of the control they have over their lives. According to learned helplessness theory, depression and its associated mental conditions can result from defeat, failure, and a person's consequent loss of control over a situation.

It is easy to remain constricted by our former experiences, failing to recognize and realize our God-given potential. But consider Saint Paul's words: "Nay, in all these things we are more than conquerors through him that loved us" (Rom. 8:37).

Psychologists have conducted hundreds of studies that have confirmed the learned helplessness phenomenon, and further research indicates that this self-defeating mind-set is reversible. People can be taught to think differently about the reasons for their prior failures. When they are shown the effectiveness of their own actions, they begin to see they have the power to make a difference.

We don't want to feel helpless and out of control. We are wired with the desire for choice, but we often do not know how to do it very well. Nevertheless, we are inclined to believe if choice is good, then more choice must be better. Sheena Iyengar has proven many of us wrong with her famous "jam study," completed while she was a doctoral student at Stanford.

Customers were offered a taste of jams at a booth set up in a neighborhood grocery store. The jams were set up in a set of six and another set of twenty-four flavors. The researchers discovered no matter how many jams they offered for sampling, on average, customers restricted their tasting to two flavors. More than half of the customers were attracted to the larger assortment, but only a handful of those made a purchase, while almost one third of the people who sampled the small assortment decided to buy jam. All those beautiful jams were appealing but paralyzing.

We've all experienced the confusion and overwhelmingness of too many choices. Often we end up putting off the decision, deciding instead not to choose—a choice to relinquish control.

Three Questions

> "Let thine hand help me; for I have chosen thy
> precepts." (Ps. 119:173)

When we are faced with the big choices, the alternatives can appear infinite or nonexistent. In either case, our response can be paralysis. We are stopped in our tracks, stymied by questions of right and wrong. What constitutes a constructive as opposed to a destructive choice about those highly consequential matters, those challenges that involve our core values and principles? Are there basic guidelines that will help ensure we make the *right* choices? How do we go about making the choices Our Designer would have us make?

I have had many opportunities to make right and wrong choices, and over the years, I have developed a simple and highly effective system that helps in the process. This story illustrates how the three basic third grade questions come into play in the COPING Strategy.

One morning, I was driving on the interstate to an appointment. All was well until a glance at my rearview mirror revealed an impatient individual driving way too close to my back bumper. All of us, including the most saintly, have hot buttons, and someone riding my bumper when I have barely removed the sleep from my eyes constitutes a hot-button moment for me. My immediate inclination was to tap my brake to send a message to that dangerous driver behind me. But first, I asked myself, *What am I doing?*

That question forced me to take ownership of my behavior, which caused me to shift my focus from what he was doing to what I was doing. When I took responsibility for my own behavior, a more constructive process began to take shape. I realized I was traveling too slowly down the interstate in the left lane—the passing lane—and impeding the flow of traffic as a result. I also became aware of the fact that I was allowing the behavior of the driver behind me to stress me, running my blood pressure up and flooding my body with stress chemicals.

I examined my behavior and asked the second question, *Is it helping?* The truthful answer was an obvious "No." If I had tapped my brake as I wanted to, I could have potentially placed myself, the driver behind me, and others in a very dangerous situation.

Next I asked myself, *What can I do that will help?* Clearly trying to teach the other driver to drive responsibly was not going to help, but I could switch into the right lane and allow him to pass. That would be helpful. I switched on my signal instead of tapping on the brake and moved over to the right lane, saying a prayer for him and those traveling around us.

I cannot say that I have always responded so admirably, but I have found that when I exercise my power of choice in a constructive way, I relax and life goes better. Sometimes, of course, "What can I do that will help?" becomes a tough question that involves ambiguity regarding right and wrong.

When I began my studies in counseling psychology at the university in the mid-1970s, much of the literature was devoid of references to right and wrong. Addressing issues of morality within the context of a therapeutic relationship was deemed inappropriate by many professionals in the field. Given my Judeo-Christian background, trying to create a helping relationship with others in need without helping them make value judgments seemed counterintuitive. Then I learned about a new approach to conventional psychotherapy, later coined *choice theory*, which recognized the importance of addressing issues of right and wrong.

Psychiatrist William Glasser incorporated choice theory into his practice with great success, and I adapted much of what I learned from him to fit my own evolving eclectic approach. The three basic third grade questions, essential to the COPING Strategy, are a direct result of his influence.

I have found that if I can communicate my ideas to a typical third grader, I probably have a good understanding of what I am trying to say, and these questions fit the bill. They provide practical guidelines that can lead us to make the right choices. I encourage you to commit them to memory for quick reference when you are faced with choices in your everyday life:

- What am I doing?

- Is it helping?

- If it is not helping, then what can I do that will help?

The first question "What am I doing?" is critical because it makes you aware of your behavior—in the moment. If you are not aware of what you are doing, it is not possible to deal with it effectively.

The second question "Is it helping?" makes a value judgment about the appropriateness of *your* behavior, not someone else's. This is the moment you recognize that, although you may have some influence over others, essentially you can only exert control over your own behavior. That is your area of responsibility.

If the answer to the second question is "Yes, it is helping," keep going. However, if the answer is "No," that is a red light. Consider stopping what you are doing and initiating a more constructive choice.

Here the third question comes into play: "If it isn't helping, what can I do that will help?" Often simply asking makes you aware of one or more appropriate alternatives, but there will be times when the answer is elusive.

Sometimes, it feels as if you have tried everything you know to do and nothing has helped. This is the time to explore resources beyond yourself. Talk to your spouse, a trusted friend, your pastor, priest, rabbi, physician, or a counselor. You might also find valuable information on the Internet, at the library, and through community agencies. Above all, ask for God's guidance, and listen.

The Ultimate Life Principle

"Most of all, let love guide your life . . ."
(Col. 3:14 TLB)

The question "Is it helping?" brings us face-to-face with our value judgments. What are we using to guide us? I choose God's Word as my compass for navigation throughout the terrain that we call life. For Christians, the knowledge of virtue and true north—our values—are contained within the teachings of Jesus, and they drive our consequential choices.

According to the scriptures, there is one principle that reigns above all others: love. "Most of all, let love guide your life . . ." (Col. 3:14 TLB). Applying the Love Principle has been an easy act in relationships with those who have been loving in their interactions with me. But like everyone else, not all of my relationships have been ideal.

A number of years ago, I entered into a business relationship with a friend and respected leader in my community. I trusted this person with a substantial portion of my financial resources, and many of my closest friends did too. Ultimately, our trust was violated when this person acted in irresponsible ways that brought much pain to many, including me. I grieved. I became physically ill. I was angry and conflicted.

In the midst of my pain and anger, I knew that the Love Principle required me to forgive my friend. But painful emotions made forgiveness a seemingly insurmountable task. In the midst of my struggle, I got down on my knees and asked God to help me do what I could not do.

That which I could not do by myself, He enabled me to do with His help. Though it was not easy, this process ultimately brought me freedom and opportunity. I vividly remember feeling sorry for myself, and then I began to imagine how Jesus felt when He was treated unfairly by those He loved. He separated them from their behavior, continued to love them, and ultimately gave His life for them and for me so that we could have eternal life. My self-pity turned to overwhelming gratitude. It was a moment of transformation.

Forgiveness freed me from the bondage of bitterness and afforded me the opportunity to share this testimony with you. I am reminded that God loves each of us while we are still sinners (Rom. 5:8) and, in doing so, separates us from our behavior. Although He loves us, He hates the sin. This separation of the person and the behavior is modeled by Jesus when a woman who was caught in the act of adultery was brought before Him for judgment. After her accusers withdrew, Jesus addressed the woman: "Neither do I condemn thee: go, and sin no more" (John 8:11).

The question "Is it helping?" challenges you to make a value judgment about behavior, not to judge others. Three more questions will help you in this regard:

- If I do this, will it enhance my relationship with God?

- If I do this, will it enhance my relationship with myself?

- If I do this, will it enhance my relationship with others?

Think of any challenging situation on an individual, societal, or global level that could not be dealt with constructively if these questions were asked. In all your dealings, keep the Love Principle at the front of your mind, and reference the Christian virtues:

> [A]dd to your faith virtue; and to virtue knowledge; And to knowledge temperance; and to temperance patience; and to patience godliness; And to godliness brotherly kindness; and to brotherly kindness charity. . . . for if ye do these things, ye shall never fall . . . (2 Peter 1:5–7, 10)

These virtues require us to behave toward others as we would have them behave toward us. However, we are not required to subject ourselves to irresponsible behavior or to condone such behavior. For example, when the religious leaders of the day were questioning Jesus regarding His followers and His teachings, He responded with great assertiveness:

Why askest thou me? ask them which heard
me, what I have said unto them: behold,
they know what I said. And when he had
thus spoken, one of the officers which stood
by struck Jesus with the palm of his hand,
saying, Answerest thou the high priest so?
Jesus answered him, If I have spoken evil,
bear witness of the evil: but if well, why
smitest thou me? (John 18:21–23)

Sometimes, being assertive is not the best course of action. The answer to the question "Is it helping?" may be a resounding "No" when you are dealing with a boss who can fire you or a friend who is too down to handle it. There are instances when assertiveness can do more harm than good.

But there are many times in our lives when assertive responses are the most responsible ones. Consider the young woman at a social function who is offered an alcoholic beverage. She would prefer not to accept the drink, but what can she do that will help? She could choose to be aggressive and instruct her host on the negative effects of alcohol. On the other hand, she could choose to accept passively and consume the beverage offered, compromising her principles. Or, she might choose an assertive response: "I'm aware that you are a considerate and gracious host who wants everyone here to have a good time, but I don't drink alcoholic beverages. Consequently, I would be most grateful if you would get me a Coke."

I refer to this as the ABC Assertiveness Model: Acknowledge the other person's point of view, state your own point of view, and express your desired outcome. This approach is assertive rather than aggressive or passive. Memorizing these words—"I am Aware . . . But . . . Consequently . . ."— and prefacing your statements with them lets you fill in the blanks so you are not searching for the right words in a stressful or uncomfortable situation.

Compensating constructively is a matter of choice. Thanks to Jesus Christ, you have the power within you to make good choices. In challenging situations, stop and ask yourself the three third grade questions: "What am I doing? Is it helping? What can I do that will help?" They will lead you to the ultimate guide for your actions, your true north—the Love Principle.

> **Consider the Choice**: What does it mean to you to choose to compensate constructively?

> **Count the Cost**: List five personal benefits of choosing to compensate constructively.

> **Claim the Promise**: What promise do you glean from the following scripture passage? "[C]hoose you this day whom ye will serve . . ." (Josh. 24:15).

Commit to the Cause: What can you do to ensure you live your life intentionally, choosing to compensate constructively?

Chapter 3

CHOOSE TO OVERCOME

"Be not overcome of evil, but overcome evil
with good." (Rom. 12:21)

Overcoming is one of the keys to greatness. It's almost
impossible to find a success story that wasn't preceded
with failures and missteps. For successful people, these are
the precursors of achievement. Overcoming is a necessary
part of the game.

Helen Keller, who was left deaf and blind by an illness
when she was just nineteen months old, is one of the world's
best-known overcomers. Thanks to her now-famous tutor,
Anne Sullivan, Helen learned how to read Braille and communicate. Against all odds, she was admitted to the presti-
gious Radcliffe College, the women's school associated with
Harvard University, where she excelled and graduated with
honors.

Helen subsequently had a remarkable writing career.
Her book *The Story of My Life* was published in 1903 and
was eventually printed in over fifty languages. Before her

death in 1968, Helen was the recipient of numerous honor-
ary degrees and awards for her humanitarian work and the
inspiration she provided to people around the world.

Helen's life could easily have gone in a much sadder direction. She could have been left isolated by her disabilities,
unschooled and unable to care for herself. Thanks to Anne
Sullivan, who showed her the way, Helen chose to overcome
rather than give up. "Life is full of suffering," Helen said. "It
is also full of the overcoming of it."

Another overcomer, Jonas Salk, tried two hundred un-
successful vaccines for polio before eventually developing
one that worked. When someone asked him how it felt to
fail all of those times, Salk reportedly responded, "I never
failed two hundred times in my life. . . . I just discovered two
hundred ways how not to vaccinate for polio."

Before Winston Churchill rose to greatness, he risked
his political career by taking an early and unpopular stand
against Hitler. He said that repeating a grade in elementary
school had prepared him to engage in such a risk. "You
mean you failed a year in grade school?" someone asked.
Churchill reportedly responded, "I never failed. . . . I was
given a second opportunity to get it right."

Failure Is Not an Event

As John Ortberg so aptly asserts in his book *If You Want to
Walk on Water, You've Got to Get Out of the Boat,* failure is
not an event. Instead, it is a judgment regarding an event.

And it is important to remember that while there are many events that escape our control, judgments involve our chosen perceptions.

Keller, Salk, and Churchill are extraordinary examples, but across thousands of years of human history, ordinary people have been subjected to an abundance of trauma, and the typical response has been resilience. Studies of survivors of traumatic events show that after a brief period of depression and anxiety, many return to their normal selves, but there is much more focus on post-traumatic stress disorder (PTSD) than post-traumatic growth (PTG).

Brigadier General Rhonda Cornum has been described as being a "poster child for post-traumatic growth." A prisoner of war during Desert Storm in 1991, Cornum is also an urologist, biochemist, flight surgeon, jet pilot, and civilian helicopter pilot. She was shot down while on a rescue mission and suffered two broken arms and a broken leg. While she was detained by Saddam Hussein's military, she was assaulted sexually and otherwise cruelly treated. After eight days, she was released and returned home a war hero.

Cornum was able to overcome her traumatic experience and go on to grow from it in ways that changed her life for the better. As a military physician, she found that after her recovery, she related better to her patients and considered herself better equipped as a leader. She also developed a better appreciation for her family, an enhanced sense of spirituality, and more focus on her most important priorities. Like Keller, she was able to turn her suffering into triumph.

Psychologist Martin Seligman has done considerable research in this area. He notes that when soldiers know only about PTSD and nothing about resilience and growth, it sets them up for a "self-fulfilling downward spiral." When they are made aware that their tears are not necessarily a symptom of PTSD but rather part of a normal grieving process, they typically become more resilient, which enables them to avoid the downward spiral. Though Seligman is concerned about the over-diagnosis of PTSD, he emphasizes his certainty that there is a "core PTSD" and that much is owed our veterans who experience it.

Self-efficacy

An account in the Old Testament illustrates the critical impact our beliefs about ourselves can have not only on ourselves but also on our families and our communities. In Numbers 13:2, God commands Moses to send a man from each tribe of Israel to search the land of Canaan, which He has given to the children of Israel. Twelve spies are selected to assess the land and its people. When these men return from their mission, they render two very contrasting reports.

This was the majority report given by ten of the spies:

> We came unto the land whither thou sentest us, and surely it floweth with milk and honey; and this is the fruit of it. Nevertheless

the people be strong that dwell in the land, and the cities are walled, and very great: and moreover we saw the children of Anak there. . . . We be not able to go up against the people; for they are stronger than we. . . . we were in our own sight as grasshoppers, and so we were in their sight. (Num. 13:27, 28, 31, 33)

The minority report was issued by Joshua and Caleb: "The land, which we passed through to search it, is an exceeding good land. If the LORD delight in us, then he will bring us into this land, and give it us; a land which floweth with milk and honey" (Num. 14:7–8). Caleb asserted, "Let us go up at once, and possess it; for we are well able to overcome it" (Num. 13:30).

Notice the language in the two reports. "We be not able" versus "we are well able." The language of the overcomer is one of self-confidence and competence based on an accurate assessment of reality. Today psychologists call it *self-efficacy*.

The children of Israel, lacking a belief in their strengths, chose to act on the majority report. Seeing themselves as grasshoppers facing giants, they sentenced themselves to forty years of wandering in the wilderness and forfeiture of their God-intended destiny (Num. 14:26–38). Their choice literally changed the course of history for an entire nation!

As the scriptures reveal, self-efficacy and self-esteem are not new concepts. People have been assessing their self-worth since Adam and Eve. While the scriptures indicate that we are "fearfully and wonderfully made" (Ps. 139:14), we are also cautioned to avoid thinking more highly of ourselves than is warranted (Rom. 12:3). Additionally, we are warned that pride precedes destruction (Prov. 16:18). Accordingly, a healthy self-assessment involves a balanced view that is consistent with how God views us—no more, but no less.

I learned something about the balanced approach to self-assessment in an embarrassing episode that dates back to my single days when I actually shopped for my own clothes. I was at the mall when I caught a beautiful woman's eye. From the moment of our first shared glance, she smiled at me radiantly. I was certain she was quite drawn to me, and I began to feel very good about myself. After more glances and even bigger smiles, I felt about ten feet tall. My self-esteem was sky-high. She disappeared before I had the chance to talk to her, but I was still walking on air when I returned to my car. One glance in the rearview mirror brought me down to earth with a great thud. What I saw was not pretty. Pasted smack dab in the middle of my forehead was a big piece of tissue. This, and not my manly good looks, had brought a smile to my "admirer." Hit squarely in the face with what I think of as a "Romans 12:3 moment," I experienced a most humbling paradigm shift.

The importance of thinking highly of ourselves—self-esteem—has been promoted in the past few decades as a panacea for individual and social ills. But more recently, self-esteem as a cure-all has its detractors. The focus has shifted in some circles from the concept of a warm and fuzzy blanket of self-esteem to greater regard for the importance of self-efficacy, which is dependent upon self-reflection but less generalized.

According to psychologist Albert Bandura, who did groundbreaking research on self-efficacy more than thirty-five years ago, self-reflection is a uniquely human ability that enables us to assess and alter our thinking and behavior. Such assessments include perceptions of self-efficacy, which he views as determining how individuals feel, think, act, and are motivated.

Bandura indicates that people with high levels of self-efficacy are prone to view difficulties as challenges to be mastered instead of threats that should be avoided. Such an outlook results in a high level of interest and engagement in activities. People with high self-efficacy typically set challenging goals for themselves and are highly committed to their accomplishments. When confronted with failure, they are apt to strengthen and sustain their efforts, and they bounce back quickly following setbacks. Instead of throwing up their hands in surrender, they are inclined to attribute their failures to a lack of effort or knowledge and skills, which they believe can be acquired. They approach threatening situations with an assurance that they have the power to overcome them. Such self-beliefs result in personal accomplishment, reduced stress, and a lowered susceptibility to depression.

Self-efficacy has both personal and social applications. Families, churches, schools, communities, and even nations develop collective beliefs regarding the capabilities of their members to perform in ways that influence the events that affect their lives. The central place self-efficacy holds in our ability to lead successful lives makes acquiring it a critical step in the COPING Strategy. So where can we find it?

As the saying goes, "Nothing builds confidence like success." And it's true. The most potent influence on self-efficacy is the experience of mastery. As people evaluate the results of their actions, they form beliefs about their competencies. On the other hand, failure has a negative effect, particularly when it's experienced at a young age, before a strong sense of efficacy has had a chance to develop. A critical aspect of mastery is that it means we have been confronted with challenge. People who aren't challenged become accustomed to achievement without sustained effort. They have no opportunity to develop self-efficacy and quickly become frustrated by their failures. The overcomers, who have had the opportunity to strengthen their self-efficacy, are much more inclined to persevere when they experience tough situations that strengthen their belief in their abilities. Helen Keller, Jonas Salk, and Winston Churchill had plenty of opportunities to experience mastery over challenges.

Another source of self-efficacy is vicarious experience. Seeing someone like yourself experience success as a result of sustained effort helps you believe you are capable of succeeding as well. That's what makes role models so important for teaching constructive ways of coping with the challenges of life. A great role model has the potential to instill self-beliefs that can change a person's destiny.

Self-efficacy is also boosted by the encouragement of others. Think of a good coach, talking up his team at half-time, pushing them past the failures of the first half. People are more likely to initiate and sustain effort with that kind of support. Without it, they doubt themselves when faced with a tough challenge. In fact, negative talk outweighs positive talk in its effect on a sense of competency. But encouragement is not enough. Effective coaches and mentors structure situations that will lead to patterns of success.

How we feel physically and emotionally impacts our sense of self-efficacy. When we're fatigued, in pain, or depressed, we don't perform as well. Repeated failures of strength, stamina, or mental clarity add up and chip away at our belief that we can succeed at the challenges we take on.

Finally, your spiritual state impacts your sense of self-efficacy in a powerful way. This spiritual dimension involves matters of faith, meaning, and purpose in life. Having a connectedness to an all-powerful God can give one a sense of control, making challenges much less threatening. Established meaning and purpose provide direction and motivate us to navigate the inevitable difficulties of life. Millions of individuals spanning many generations have been empowered to overcome seemingly insurmountable challenges as a result of their religious faith. Faith in the efficacy of the supreme sacrifice made by Jesus Christ through His death and resurrection, and the words of our Christian testimony, lift us up and enable us to be overcomers.

Competency Married to Character

The mere development of competency and an accompanying sense of self-efficacy will not yield a successful life. Competency must be married to character. Thus, we are defined not just by what we say and do, but, most importantly, by who we are.

This is a concept that has not been popular over the past few decades. Sociologists and psychologists looking at antisocial and other undesirable behaviors have tended to lay the blame on negative influences such as poverty and racism, not on character. Anna Russell illustrates this victim idea in a song that proclaims, "[E]verything I do that's wrong is someone else's fault."

In his book *Flourish*, Martin Seligman examines this shift in our culture and finds that negation of personal responsibility has replaced character as a primary explanation for undesirable behavior. As a result, we tend to identify the situations that underlie social ills and concentrate on undesirable events instead of desirable ones.

Seligman acknowledges there are certainly times when individuals are victimized by events beyond their control. But he believes bad behavior is often the result of bad choices, and that is a matter of character. When we blame events, personal responsibility and free will are often minimized or totally disregarded.

Rather than character, our society emphasizes the quick fix for personal and social problems. Positive-thinking strategies are touted as the secret of success. While these techniques and strategies can be very useful, when they trump matters of character, the end result becomes flawed.

Our educational institutions are charged with preparing one of our nation's most significant resources, our children, with the skills required to build successful lives. But a lack of achievement is rampant. Underachievement is frequently attributed to inadequate teachers, poorly written textbooks, a lack of funding, flawed politics, dysfunctional families, and a host of other factors. For quite some time, matters of personal character didn't get much attention, but the concept of individual responsibility is beginning to show up again in recent studies.

Angela Lee Duckworth, a student of Martin Seligman's at Stanford, asserts school failure results, at least in part, from the characters of failing students and not simply from a system that results in their victimization. Obviously, she has not fallen victim to the political correctness of our day. In her first-year thesis, Duckworth concluded that students often do not actualize their intellectual potential due to a demonstrated lack of self-discipline. These students have difficulty executing choices that require them to forfeit pleasure in the short-term for long-term benefits. She indicates that educational programs that foster the development of self-discipline will be ones most likely to result in students who are academically successful.

As a Christian, I turn to the Holy Scriptures for instruction and guidance on matters of character. I recognize that the virtues and principles contained in the Bible represent the best way for all people to live. Ideally, I would like everyone to embrace the Christian faith; however, I recognize that when my Jewish, Muslim, and Buddhist neighbors practice the same principles, they likely reap similar benefits.

The Apostle Peter encapsulates Christian character within a half-dozen verses and is so certain regarding such matters that he includes a written guarantee for personal success:

And beside this, giving all diligence, add to your faith virtue; and to virtue knowledge; And to knowledge temperance; and to temperance patience; and to patience godliness; And to godliness brotherly kindness; and to brotherly kindness charity. For if these things be in you, and abound, they make you that ye shall neither be barren nor unfruitful in the knowledge of our Lord Jesus Christ. But he that lacketh these things is blind, and cannot see afar off, and hath forgotten that he was purged from his old sins. Wherefore the rather, brethren, give diligence to make your calling and election sure: for if ye do these things, ye shall never fall . . . (2 Pet. 1:5-10)

The Revelation of Jesus Christ to John, in the last book of the New Testament, contains a message of triumph for the overcomers: "To him that overcometh will I give to eat of the tree of life, which is in the midst of the paradise of God" (Rev. 2:7), and "he that overcometh, and keepeth my works unto the end, to him will I give power over the nations . . . " (Rev. 2:26).

A fitting capstone of divine instruction to one who seeks to become the ultimate overcomer is contained within the following scripture: "He that overcometh shall inherit all things; and I will be his God, and he shall be my son" (Rev.

21:7).

> **Consider the Choice**: What does being an overcomer mean to you?
>
> **Count the Cost**: List five character traits you possess that are most beneficial when confronted with challenge.
>
> **Claim the Promise**: What promise do you glean from the following scripture passage? "Be not overcome of evil, but overcome evil with good" (Rom. 12:21).
>
> **Commit to the Cause**: What can you do to ensure you live your life intentionally, choosing to overcome?

Chapter 4

CHOOSE TO PAUSE TO NURTURE YOUR SPIRIT

"Be still, and know that I am God . . . "
(Ps. 46:10)

There are those who proclaim that our journey toward fulfillment leads to happiness. There certainly is much to be said for a life of happiness, but as Kay Warren professes in *Choose Joy*, happiness is never enough. Joy prevails where happiness is fleeting. Unlike happiness, it cannot be held hostage by circumstances or manipulated by people, places, or possessions. Joy drinks from a much deeper well than happiness. Its source is God. Rick Warren says joy is birthed when we place our faith in Him and resolve to praise Him through it all.

Choosing joy is not always an easy route, especially in the face of adversity. But consider the self-efficacy of individuals who assert that "the joy of the Lord" is their strength (Neh. 8:10), that joy is a manifestation of a spiritual life (Gal. 5:22), and that a state of transcendence provides opportunities to find meaning and purpose even in the face of adversity (James 1:2-3). Imagine the impact choosing joy would have on your life decisions.

Seeking Joy

Seeking joy, then, is a matter of being in close communication with God. Most Americans, unfortunately, spend so much time staring at some sort of screen that they leave little time for prayer and introspection. The average American spends eight to ten hours a day on the computer, the smartphone, or the television. The average American teenager sends or receives seventy-five text messages a day. Seventy-five! I'm not making this up. These are statistics cited in a December 29, 2011 *New York Times* article titled "The Joy of Quiet."

The joy of quiet indeed. It is a rare experience these days that too few Americans seek. "All of humanity's problems stem from man's inability to sit quietly in a room alone," declared philosopher Blaise Pascal. Saint Paul instructed us to "study to be quiet" (1 Thess. 4:11), and God commanded, "Be still and know that I am God" (Ps. 46:10). What benefits would be reaped if we decided to pause regularly in order to quietly nurture our spirits?

The Big Questions

Why are so many of us uncomfortable with quietness in our lives? Could it be that without distractions we become confronted by ourselves? Are we afraid of facing the big questions—who we are, why we are here, and where we are going?

These are spiritual questions that readily surface, given moments of quiet seclusion from the onslaughts of our modern lives. Developing a spiritual life that invites meditation and prayer is a highly effective way to create this necessary quiet space for ourselves.

An abundance of research has shown that spirituality, religious belief, and practice, including prayer and meditation, decrease the incidence of disease, enhance the rate of recovery from illnesses, and result in longer life. Studies indicate that individuals who attend church regularly generally benefit from better health and live longer, while people who seldom attend religious services are more likely to die from circulatory, digestive, and respiratory disorders.

The benefits of religious involvement, including social interaction and support that encourage a healthy lifestyle, have a direct impact on stress and life management. Spiritual resources provide a sense of hope, meaning, and support that help individuals cope with stress more effectively, according to an article in the American Psychological Association's publication *Monitor*.

One of the basic teachings from much of the wisdom literature throughout the world is that each life is part of a much greater whole. In Christ, Christians are a part of the family of God, the God to whom all power belongs, who loves them, and who has a specific plan for their lives. This knowledge nurtures a sense of meaning and purpose in their lives and impacts the choices they make at the most significant crossroads.

As we grow older, despite achieving and acquiring much, many of us experience an intensified thirst for meaning and purpose. We begin to ask the big questions: Who am I? Why am I here? Where am I going? Psychiatrist and concentration camp survivor Viktor Frankl observed that many people have enough to live on but nothing to live for. They have "the means, but no meaning." Even in a world of abundance, for so many, happiness has remained elusive. "Never have so many had so much and enjoyed it so little," I once heard someone say.

A visit to the landfill provides a powerful object lesson as one surveys the collection and tries to imagine the individual stories behind each of the items discarded. Did that old couch once grace the parlor of an opulent mansion? Perhaps that was a little girl's first bicycle. Was that the fender of a luxury car involved in a fatal accident? Is that wrapping from a birthday present? Imagine how many games that old baseball bat saw before it was retired. No matter where they came from or who cherished them, these items shared a destiny—the landfill. What is the purpose of all of this stuff?

Since its publication in 2002, *The Purpose-Driven Life* by Rick Warren has become the bestselling hardcover nonfiction book in history other than the Bible, having sold tens of millions of copies worldwide. The incredible success of this book exemplifies our intensified hunger for meaning and purpose in our lives.

Warren challenges the conventional self-help advice that suggests we must begin by searching within ourselves, examining our own desires and aspirations for ultimate purpose and meaning in life. Citing over twelve hundred scriptural references, Warren relates that we were created by God for His purposes, and until we understand this, our thirst for meaning and purpose will not be quenched.

I couldn't agree more. The teachings of Jesus indicate that all of us share a God-given purpose. The Great Commandment and the Great Commission sum up this purpose:

The Great Commandment

> Thou shalt love the Lord thy God with all thy heart, and with all thy soul, and with all thy mind. This is the first and great commandment.
>
> And the second is like unto it, Thou shalt love thy neighbor as thyself. On these two commandments hang all the law and the prophets. (Matt. 22:37–40)

The Great Commission

> And Jesus came and spake unto them, saying, All power is given unto me in heaven and in earth. Go ye therefore, and teach all nations, baptizing them in the name of the Father, and of the Son, and of the Holy Ghost: Teaching them to observe all things whatsoever I have commanded you: and, lo, I am with you always, even unto the end of the world. Amen. (Matt. 28:18–20)

In addition to our shared mission, God created us as individuals with unique gifts and abilities to accomplish His purpose. In Romans 12:4–6, Saint Paul relates that as Christians we are "many members in one body," with various members serving different functions having "gifts differing according to the grace that is given to us."

Personalizing the Mission

What are your unique gifts and abilities? What experiences have prepared you to be more effective in accomplishing that which yields meaning and purpose? What is your personal testimony? The answers to these questions can help clarify your personal mission in life.

The word *mission* comes from a Latin word that means "sending." As followers of Jesus Christ, we have been sent into the world to be His ambassadors (John 20:21). As such, we have been given personal assignments that are not optional. God-given missions are awesome privileges and tremendous responsibilities. What could be more rewarding than helping other people initiate eternal relationships with God, ones that shape their destinies and empower them to discover the ultimate meaning and purpose of their lives?

I had this privilege with my birth mother, Norma. I always ended our phone conversations with the same routine. "Remember, we should make sure that our relationship with the Lord is what it ought to be," I would say. "So you say your prayers for me, and I'll say mine for you."

It usually served its purpose well by easing my conscience. With this brief, non-confrontational exchange, I assured myself I'd done my part to employ the Great Commission in my relationship with Norma. But the time came when this approach did not feel right. At the end of another one of our conversations, my spirit objected as loudly as if a presiding judge had banged his gavel. I knew that it was time to initiate a different approach. Without hesitation, I gently but boldly asked, "Norma, have you ever given your heart to the Lord?"

She knew exactly what I was asking. Following a brief hesitation, she said, "No."

"Would you like to?"

"Yes."

I talked with her about the "ABCs of Being in Him," as indexed in Appendix B of this publication. Then we prayed a sinner's prayer.

Wow! Apparently, I had just helped my biological mother into the Kingdom of God!

It was one of the greatest feelings in the world. But that was a lofty assignment that could seem intimidating and overwhelming. Perhaps we suffer from what psychologist Abraham Maslow called the *Jonah complex* in our inability or unwillingness to actualize our God-given potentials in such areas.

Like many of us, Jonah was hesitant to carry out his God-given mission. He was charged with going to Nineveh to warn the people to repent. But because this was one of the last places he wanted to go, he boarded a ship and headed in the opposite direction. The ship encountered a storm, and its crew threw Jonah overboard. After spending three days inside the belly of "a great fish," he had a change of heart. After being upchucked by the fish onto dry land, he went to Nineveh and delivered God's warning.

Maslow believed that we fear our best as much as we fear our worst. Some of us are afraid of being perceived as immodest and extreme. We stifle initiative as we embrace a fabricated humility and set low goals for ourselves. Many of us are petrified at the thought of making a remarkable impact upon the world around us because we fear the possibility of the attention it would draw.

The Jonah complex also involves a fear of loss of control. It can be disconcerting to think that we may experience a total transformation as a result of embracing our true potential and ultimate mission in life. The paradox is that letting go brings freedom and opportunity.

Many Christians prefer acting on the Great Commission through "silent witness," a way to share Christian witness by modeling Christian behavior. They view it as less intimidating than a more direct approach. Though silent witness can be very effective, it doesn't harness the incredible power of the story.

Stories have always been part of the human experience. Even before language developed, stories were told in pictures scratched on the walls of caves. There is no record of any great society that didn't have stories. Stories perpetuate cultures. They transmit values and principles from one generation to another.

Stories link language and emotion, which creates a great impact. It's difficult to remember a list of facts, but when those facts are embedded in a story told with passion, we are more likely to remember. Actions speak louder than words. The story combines the two. Add emotion, and your story becomes a powerful witness for Jesus Christ. Think of the power your own story carries. Does it have the potential to encourage someone or even transform a life?

Three people were competing in a race to complete a one thousand-piece jigsaw puzzle. The first person was given a box with a picture of the puzzle on the front of the box. The second person was given a box without a picture on it. The third person was given a box with the wrong picture on the front of it. It's not difficult to predict who won that race, and so it is in our lives. Without a clear picture of what we want to accomplish in life, the journey will be most challenging: "Where there is no vision, the people perish: but he that keepeth the law, happy is he" (Prov. 29:18). When people do not pursue a vision consistent with God's will for their lives, doing their own thing instead without a sense of unity in purpose and direction, destruction is inevitable.

In 1968, Martin Luther King defined his vision in one of the most famous speeches of all time. His "I Have a Dream" speech resonated then and now in ways that have resulted in a better world. Most vision statements do not have such a broad impact, but when they are based on core values, every one has the potential to change lives.

A vision statement defines what we want to accomplish, and a mission statement defines more specifically what we intend to do in order to bring this vision to fruition. A personal mission statement is a clear and concise proclamation that defines your purpose in life. It provides you with your own customized GPS, keeping you on track and focused on your vision. It is a statement driven by core values, a personal constitution that incites motivation and focused direction. Your mission statement distinguishes what you will embrace from what you won't. In it, you join who you are called to be with what you have been prepared to do.

Let us consider the mission statement of Jesus, proclaimed in His hometown synagogue. He quotes the words of Isaiah:

> The Spirit of the Lord is upon me, because he hath anointed me to preach the gospel to the poor; he hath sent me to heal the broken-hearted, to preach deliverance to the captives, and recovering of sight to the blind, to set at liberty them that are bruised, To preach the acceptable year of the Lord. (Luke 4:18–19)

Here are some practical suggestions to consider when developing your own personal mission statement:

- Begin by asking God in your prayer time to reveal His specific plan for your life.

- Read and meditate upon the scriptures, especially those that are relevant to God's intended purpose for all of our lives.

- Review other appropriate resources, such as *The Purpose-Driven Life* by Rick Warren and *First Things First* by Stephen R. Covey, A. Roger Merrill, and Rebecca Merrill.

- Write your thoughts on paper.

- Consider the impact this statement will have on your life. Don't rush it.

- Make a list of your God-given gifts and abilities.

- Contemplate "The Big Three"—Who am I? Why am I here? Where am I going?

- List five to nine core values that you want to guide you in making the most consequential choices in life.

- Think about what energizes you. What invokes your deepest passions?

- Focus on a life lived for something larger than yourself, targeting your service to God through your service to others.

- Contemplate how you would invest your time if you knew you had only this year to live.

- Identify who your intended audience will be.

Aspire to write a brief but strong mission statement— brief enough to remember but strong enough to inspire. Recognize that your mission statement is not a to-do list or a job description. It is a living proclamation that you will internalize to the extent that it will govern all choices.

Write this statement upon your heart and review it regularly. There may come a time when you want to revise it. That's fine. This is a living document, one that will guide your life.

When our actions are congruent with our values, our lives are much less stressful. A mission statement reflects these core values. It reveals what makes us tick. It proclaims what we would live and die for. These values are the navigational system by which we negotiate the most consequential choices of our lives. When they are well-defined, decision making is simplified and more efficient. From these essential values, our mission statements are born, and our statements in turn energize our core values, bringing them to action and directing them toward an ultimate purpose. When we tap into the core of who we are, which is our character, and consider what we are capable of doing, which is our sense of efficacy, we set the stage for an explosion of passion that becomes the unique fingerprint of our lives. As we become conscious of the potential contributions we can make, we are given direction and energy we didn't realize we possessed. We are inspired to dream and to consider what can be.

An anonymous wise person once said, "As you climb the ladder of success, check occasionally to make sure it is leaning against the right wall."

- Your vision statement defines which wall you want to climb.

- Your core values define which ladder you will use to climb the wall.

- Your mission statement defines how you will climb that wall with this ladder.

Here is my personal vision statement: "My dream is to inspire and empower children and adults all over the world to make choices that will enhance their relationships with God, themselves, and others." This is my personal mission statement: "My dream to inspire and empower others will be accomplished by sharing the COPING Strategy with thousands of individuals throughout the world via the means accorded me, including spoken, written, and electronic media." Having read these two statements, you know what makes me tick, gives my life direction, and fuels my ultimate passions.

Structuring my days to include pausing regularly during private times in order to nurture my spirit has helped to keep me centered upon my vision and mission statements, as well as on the core values upon which they are based. During such times, I use the ACTS model when I talk with God in my personal devotions, expressing my ADORATION of Him, CONFESSING any sin that may be in my life, and offering THANKSGIVING for His favor and blessings before sharing my SUPPLICATION or requests (Phil. 4:6). Addressing my supplication to Him, I ask Him to help me that day to choose to compensate constructively, choose to overcome, choose to pause, choose to initiate, choose to negate negative thinking, and choose to give. I encourage you to memorize this supplication and practice it often. It is the heart of this book, containing the keys to living a life of wholeness in a broken world. Accordingly, these are six of the most important choices we could ever make and encourage others to make.

As a Christian striving to live a life of wholeness in a broken world, it is easy to become distracted by all the weighty stuff and forget how very much I have to be thankful for. I find it helps to have an object in my surroundings that serves as a reminder. Joshua was aware of the importance of physical reminders of God's faithfulness when he explained to the Israelites the purpose of stones of remembrance:

> Then Joshua explained again the purpose of the stones: "In the future," he said, "when your children ask you why these stones are here and what they mean, you are to tell them that these stones are a reminder of this amazing miracle—that the nation of Israel crossed the Jordan River on dry ground! Tell them how the Lord our God dried up the river right before our eyes, and then kept it dry until we were all across! It is the same thing the Lord did forty years ago at the Red Sea! He did this

so that all the nations of the earth will realize
that Jehovah is the mighty God, and so that
all of you will worship him forever." (Josh.
4:21–24 TLB)

Inspired by Joshua, I purchased a large and beautiful
rainbow rock indigenous to Turkey, which I had delivered
to our house. It is positioned in a prominent place in the
landscape beside our driveway. This is my stone of remembrance of God's many blessings. What this stone represents
nurtures my inner self and energizes me, as well as others
with whom I share its significance.

> **Consider the Choice**: How much private time
> are you willing to devote each day to pausing and
> nurturing your spirit?

> **Count the Cost**: What are some advantages of
> choosing to pause regularly and disadvantages of
> choosing not to do so?

> **Claim the Promise**: What promise do you glean
> from the following scripture passage? "Be still, and
> know that I am God . . . " (Ps. 46:10).

> **Commit to the Cause**: What can you do to ensure
> you live your life intentionally, choosing to pause?

Chapter 5

CHOOSE TO INITIATE

"In the beginning, God. . . ."
(Gen. 1:1)

A successful, rewarding life is built by a series of beginnings. Our mission statements point the way to the actions we will initiate. When the moment is right, we must act, but first, we must wait. When waiting is the constructive thing to do, it is a very active process that is initiated with intention.

Play the Rests

My pastor, who is a gifted pianist, related a story that illustrates the importance of waiting. His childhood piano teacher used to tell him, "Always remember to play the rests!"

Musical scores consist of time signatures that define rhythm and beat. Notes represent tones to be played or sung. Bar lines divide measures of music. In addition to these notations, there are ones called "rests." When a rest is indicated on the score, the vocalist stops singing, the pianist's fingers no longer touch the keyboard, the violinist stills the strings, the horn player doesn't blow, and the drummer lifts his sticks from the skins. It's time to contemplate what came before, experience the moment, and anticipate what is yet to come.

"But they that wait upon the LORD shall renew their strength; they shall mount up with wings as eagles; they shall run, and not be weary; and they shall walk, and not faint" (Isa. 40:31). This is a passage familiar to most Christians, yet many of us run with weariness and walk in fainthearted-ness. Why is this? Could it be that we have not mastered the art of waiting in the manner that God intended?

In his book *Broken Bread*, John Follette encourages us to take a closer look at this passage. He points out that the blessings God promises are contingent on waiting upon the Lord. Thus, if we are not experiencing the promised blessings, it follows that either we have not met the required condition or we do not comprehend its meaning.

So what does God mean when He tells us to "wait upon the Lord?" The word *waiting* is referenced many times in the Bible, and there are many shades of meaning. Follette has classified these many uses of the word into four general categories. The initial meaning of the word is "silence." This involves quieting our body, soul, and spirit after our prayers have been made. It is a time set aside when we silently bow before God. I have a friend who describes her times of silence before God as "climbing into His lap." These are times following her prayers when she submits herself totally to God and experiences His nurturance as she draws close to Him in intimate moments of quietness.

We live out our lives in worlds of seismic noise and activity that often spill over into our spirits, infecting them in ways that can be harmful to their development. Silencing ourselves before God with intention, our faith is activated as we quietly wait in God's presence. It is a time during which miracles are wrought by Him.

We pray for miracles, but we often forego the waiting. Many of us spend time pouring our petitions out to God, hurriedly dismissing Him as we rush out of His presence and go off and do things our own way. What if we taught our children to say their prayers and then taught them to hush their spirits as they remained in His presence?

A second meaning of waiting is "expectation and hope." It is waiting of this sort that develops our dependence on a power that transcends ourselves. During such times, self-sufficiency is negated. Rather, we grow in the realization that our ultimate expectation and hope is in Him. It is these first two meanings of waiting that are most related to our choice to pause in order to nurture our spirits. What if after we taught our children to pray and hush their spirits, we also taught them that their expectations and hopes rest in Him?

A third meaning of waiting is "watching, observing, taking notice." Taken in this sense, we are instructed to be close and focused upon Him in order to perceive His will. Waiting helps us discern the still, small voice that speaks to us inwardly. Qualifying all we do through His Word that He has revealed to us in the Holy Scriptures is paramount here. What if we taught our children to watch Him so closely that they are able to perceive His will for their lives?

The fourth meaning of waiting is "to serve or minister." The story related in the twenty-third chapter of 2 Samuel illustrates this meaning. Although David had many mighty men who served him, three of them were elevated above all the others. They were granted favored positions because they knew how to wait in this fourth sense of the word. David had not yet ascended to the throne as king and was being pursued by his enemies. A garrison of the Philistines was in nearby Bethlehem. He sighed and said quietly, "Oh, that one would give me drink of the water of the well of Bethlehem, which is by the gate!" The three men heard David's wish and penetrated the host of Philistines to draw water out of the well by the gate. Then the men fought their way back and took the water to David. These three men were close enough and quiet enough to hear David's longing, which they seized as an opportunity to serve him.

What if we taught our children to look for opportunities to serve and minister on His behalf? And what if the primary means of our teaching involved consistently modeling these activities? What would the benefits be? How valuable would this legacy be?

There are times when waiting is simply the most constructive thing to do. For example, times when you are emotionally distraught are not the best times to make long-term decisions. Impulsivity can also result in impaired judgment. In some situations, delaying gratification can lead to a more constructive choice. Ask yourself, "If I do this, is it going to help? Is waiting the most constructive thing to do, or am I waiting because I want someone else to take over my responsibility?"

Instant versus Delayed Gratification

We live in a culture that promotes instant gratification. "I want it now!" says a character in a popular television commercial. Whether it's the child in the classroom who has difficulty waiting for his turn to answer or the adult who leaps to his feet to order the newer, improved model of whatever. "But wait! If you call now, you can receive two for the price of one!" Impulsivity often rules the day.

A Duke University study involving over one thousand New Zealand children found that children as young as three years old who demonstrated lower degrees of self-control were more likely to experience health issues, drug problems, difficulties with money management, and violations of the law almost thirty years later. Wow! How do we quantify the physical, psychological, spiritual, and financial costs of these children's inability to wait?

Another famous research study into delayed gratification was conducted by Dr. Walter Mischel, who completed a landmark study at Stanford University. Children were placed in a room with a marshmallow and were given the choice to eat it either then or fifteen minutes later. If they chose to wait, they were promised a second marshmallow as a reward. In a follow-up study ten years later, researchers found that children who had been able to delay their gratification were more successful as adults than those who had consumed their marshmallows immediately.

These studies indicate that the ability to delay gratification is a cornerstone to building a productive life. Researchers reported that the children who delayed longer in the marshmallow experiments proved to be planful, resourceful in initiating activities, trustworthy, self-assertive, and concerned about moral values. Each of these characteristics is fundamentally related to the principles found within the COPING Strategy.

The good news is that self-control can be learned. Even at a young age, people can be taught to change their attitudes toward gratification. They can develop decision-making skills and learn to recognize the long-term consequences of their chosen actions.

Managing Your Time

When waiting is not the constructive thing to do, procrastination becomes the thief of time. Dealing constructively with the matter of procrastination means choosing to redeem and invest our time, which brings us to the subject of time management. Of course, we can't control the passage of time. Here the king and the pauper are on equal footing. Everyone gets twenty-four hours a day and 365 days a year. While we cannot manage the amount of time we are given, we can manage our behavior in relation to time.

Many people find they get more done in less time using various time-management methods, such as notes and checklists, planners and appointment books, and an assortment of paper-based and electronic devices. But they often find that their increased productivity is at the expense of the enriched relationships and inner peace that accompany doing those things that matter most in life.

Manage your life choices with the aid of a so-called compass that points to "true north" is the advice of Stephen Covey, A. Roger Merrill, and Rebecca Merrill in *First Things First*. Such choices are driven by principles instead of the urgency of the clock. When we prioritize according to our true north, we become empowered, and our lives are enhanced, along with the lives of those with whom we are involved.

The authors of *First Things First* suggest that we combine traditional time-management methods with the true-north concept, which favors importance over urgency. For Christians, these true-north principles are both universal and timeless truths that are anchored in God. They work anytime, anywhere, with anyone. Incorporating these principles into our approach to planning is more about life management than time management.

With our "hurry-up-and-get-it-done" and "bottom line" attitudes, we often seek quick fixes that consist of lists of steps. These make us feel better because they tell us what to do regardless of the situation. But particular actions are not always appropriate in every situation, for every individual or group, at every given time.

Consider the kindergartener who removed a handgun from his backpack at school and was suspended from that institution in accordance with prescribed actions to be taken in such cases. While this was definitely a situation that had to be dealt with immediately, should it have made a difference that the handgun was placed without his knowledge in this child's backpack by his older brother? If the resulting disciplinary action had been based on principles of fairness and personal responsibility rather than on a rigid set of rules, would the boy have been tossed out of his school?

When we internalize the principles we base our actions on and share them with others through modeling and other means, we equip ourselves to deal effectively with the inevitable challenges that stand in our way. This approach requires an investment of our time and energy but yields countless benefits in the lives of our children, ourselves, and others with whom we interact.

When It's Time to Act

I once worked with a particularly intelligent and talented woman. Her ability to formulate plans to address challenges brought before our organization was impressive. But I noticed that after she submitted her plans, she did not implement them. Consequently, to the extent that they involved her investment, her plans failed because they were not initiated. It's easy to empathize with her because most of us have experienced those times when we had keen insight and direction but could not muster the "unction" to function!

"A journey of a thousand miles must begin with a single step," wrote the Chinese philosopher Lao Tzu. "The beginning is the most important part of the work," said the Greek philosopher Plato. The American writer W. Clement Stone said, "So many fail because they don't get started—they don't go. They don't overcome inertia. They don't begin." And there's the rub.

Another word for *begin* is "initiate." In *Beyond Talent*, author John Maxwell describes talent as a God-given gift that you should celebrate, but he declares that talent is never enough. It is the choices you make that take you far beyond your talent, enabling you to become a "talent-plus person." Maxwell indicates that those who lack initiative often do not recognize the consequences of their inactivity. Consequently, they fail to execute right choices on their own initiative. In contrast, the "talent-plus person" does not fall prey to this deception.

Motivational speaker and author Joachim de Posada looks at initiative from another angle. He has added a qualification to the statement "Knowledge is power." He submits, "Applied knowledge is power." He describes three frogs floating down a river on top of a leaf. One of the frogs decides to jump off. Posada asks, "How many frogs are left?" Most people answer that two frogs remain on the leaf. But he states that three frogs still remain on top of the leaf. How can this be? Deciding to jump and jumping are not the same thing.

Why is it so hard for so many of us to jump? And why are the most constructive choices in our lives so difficult to execute? We are aware that spending more time in prayer and Bible study is a priority for our spiritual well-being. We know that monitoring our diets more closely and exercising regularly will improve our health. We recognize the benefits of spending more time nurturing the significant relationships in our lives. We decide to do these and other important things with the noblest of intentions. But much too often, we procrastinate.

James, the half-brother of Jesus, says, "Even so faith, if it hath not works, is dead. . . ." (James 2:17) and "[B]e ye doers of the word, and not hearers only. . . ." (James 1:22). In his letter to the Colossians, Saint Paul urges them to make wise choices, "redeeming the time" (Col. 4:5). The Latin phrase *carpe diem* means "seize the day," warning us to make the most constructive use of the finite amount of time that we have.

One of the most incredible stories in the New Testament speaks to the absolute necessity of seizing the day. It illustrates the phenomenal power of initiation—choosing to begin when it is time to start:

> And in the fourth watch of the night Jesus went unto them, walking on the sea. And when the disciples saw him walking on the sea, they were troubled, saying, It is a spirit; and they cried out for fear. But straightway Jesus spake unto them, saying, Be of good cheer; it is I; be not afraid. And Peter answered him and said, Lord, if it be thou, bid me come unto thee on the water. And he said, Come. And when Peter was come down out of the ship, he walked on the water, to go to Jesus. But when he saw the wind boisterous, he was afraid; and beginning to sink, he cried, saying, Lord, save me. And immediately Jesus stretched forth his hand,

and caught him, and said unto him, O thou
of little faith, wherefore didst thou doubt?
And when they were come into the ship, the
wind ceased. (Matt. 14:25–32)

John Ortberg elaborates on this story in *If You Want to
Walk on Water, You've Got to Get Out of the Boat*. The takeaway message is that if we want to have God's power op-
erating in our lives, we cannot be sedentary. Rather, living
our lives consistent with His Word requires initiative. This
means moving when it is time to begin and waiting actively
when it is time to pause. This is the kind of action that is
the result of saying yes to God and trusting Him to take the
utmost care of you.

It is easy to focus on Peter's lack of faith and consequential sinking. But if we do, we fail to recognize that eleven
individuals remained in the boat, choosing to be spectators
rather than active participants in this divine event. Ortberg
refers to such individuals as "boat potatoes," whose major
liability is a lack of growth.

Peter is not the impulsive risk-taker among the boat
potatoes. He does not dive into the water in the midst of a
violent storm. Rather, before he chooses to leave the safety
of the boat, he makes sure Jesus thinks this is an appropriate
choice. Then when he hears Jesus say, "Come," Peter gets
out of the boat and walks on the water toward his Lord.
He begins to sink only when he becomes distracted and
intimidated by the boisterous wind.

A number of years ago, I attended a large church meeting with my father. The speaker was an internationally known evangelist, and his opening remarks immediately captured the audience's attention: "I will prove that Peter did not walk on the water." The evangelist stressed that Peter's story was primarily one of obedience. Being a mere man, he said, it was impossible for Peter to walk on the water. Rather, he walked on the Word of his Lord—"Come."

As a Christian, I actively seek to actualize God's will in my life by listening to His Word as revealed in the Holy Scriptures. Although I have never heard the audible voice of God, there have been times when, through prayer and meditation, I have sought and come to know His will. Those are the times when I have been assured it was safe to get out of my boat. Developing, implementing, and presenting the COPING Strategy has involved getting out of my boat and trusting God to enable me to impart a message to others that without Him I could not do.

There was a time during my career as a school psychologist when applying this key principle in the COPING Strategy yielded particularly positive results. My colleagues and I had become increasingly concerned about the need for counseling services for students and their families in our community who could not afford the expense. After lamenting the lack of available alternatives, we chose to practice what we were preaching and apply the COPING Strategy to this challenging situation. That's how the free clinic was born.

We got out of our boat. My colleagues, Dr. Dennis Todd and Pauline Gregory, volunteered their excellent counseling services. The school board provided facilities. School personnel, especially guidance counselors, made referrals. Our secretary made the appointments and also volunteered to provide childcare services. I was afforded the opportunity to present the COPING Strategy to clients, and it was implemented in their therapeutic plans. The impact of that act of initiation a number of years ago continues to resonate in ways beyond measure for those who received our services and for us.

Can you think of a time when you had the courage to get out of your boat and something absolutely incredible happened? Perhaps more importantly, what is your boat? What is it that your life is anchored to aside from God? Thought provoking, isn't it?

Dealing with Procrastination Tomorrow

Have there been times when you intended to get out of your boat? Perhaps you even made elaborate plans to become involved, but you couldn't muster the unction to function. Perhaps tomorrow?

Procrastination is normal to a degree. Moderation is the key. Procrastination is abnormal when it interferes significantly with your ability to function. When it becomes chronic, brokenness is birthed.

Canadian psychologist Dr. Piers Steel is a leading expert on the subject of procrastination. Following ten years of research, Steel found those of us who are prone to procrastinate are part of a growing number. In 1978, approximately 5 percent of Americans viewed themselves as being chronic procrastinators, as contrasted with 26 percent in 2007.

Steel describes a procrastinator as "less healthy, less wealthy, and less happy." He identifies an "intention-action gap" associated with an individual's failure to act upon intentions. Other common characteristics include neglect of one's duty, a lack of purposeful planning and perseverance, as well as decreased motivation, unless tasks are intrinsically motivating.

In *The Procrastination Equation*, Steel says impulsiveness is "the core of procrastination," and without it, chronic procrastination would not exist. Research shows that procrastinators generally make plans to initiate a task just like non-procrastinators. The difference comes at the time to act upon their plans. Herein lies the intention-action gap, and its perpetrator is time. We naturally value rewards that are quickly attainable much more highly than those that require us to wait. Thus, we are impulsive. We tend to view matters pertaining to the future in relatively abstract terms, while more immediate matters of today are seen in more concrete terms. Steel says this is chiefly why we procrastinate. We are not necessarily lazy. We have good intentions, but when the future morphs into today, we just can't seem to get motivated.

So how do we go about initiating a procrastination-reduction plan? Here are some suggestions:

- Explore ways to make tasks more appealing. You might try making a boring task more difficult or piggybacking a task that has a long-term reward with one that has a more immediate reward.

- Boost your sense of self-efficacy. Watch someone with whom you identify complete the task successfully. Break challenging tasks down into small steps so you can experience successes.

- Divorce your self-worth from your performance and respect yourself for the effort you put into it.

- Reduce distractions. Study or work in a secluded and quiet area. Avoid access to e-mail, the Internet, and smartphones.

- Refuse to engage in activities that are not productive. Learn how to delegate so you can concentrate on your most productive activities.

Bad things can come to those who delay. Do you recall hearing about Elisha Gray and how he lost a fortune? I can't say that I did either. There's a reason for that. He lost credit for the invention of the telephone because he submitted his idea to the patent office minutes too late. I bet Alexander Graham rings a Bell!

Consider the Choice: Do you know when to wait and when to act?

Count the Cost: What changes are you willing to make to overcome your procrastination?

Claim the Promise: What promise do you glean from the following scripture passage? "Even so faith, if it hath not works, is dead, being alone" (James 2:17).

Commit to the Cause: What can you do to ensure that you live your life intentionally, choosing to initiate?

Chapter 6

CHOOSE TO NEGATE NEGATIVE THINKING

"For as he thinketh in his heart, so is he. . . ."
(Prov. 23:7)

The power of thought is integral to the COPING Strategy. The knowledge that positive thinking is an important tool in building success is as old as the scriptures, and when it is incorporated into the Strategy, it becomes a super power. Pastor, author, and educator Charles Swindoll sums up the concept perfectly—so perfectly that I have displayed his quote in my study for many years: "The longer I live, the more I realize the impact of attitude on my life. . . . The remarkable thing is we have a choice every day regarding the attitude we embrace for that day. . . ."

Thinking about Thinking

The average person has approximately fifty thousand thoughts each day, and getting up every morning in a positive frame of mind is one of the most constructive things we can do. The motivational speaker Zig Ziglar recommends "a checkup from the neck up."

You are in charge of your attitude. Respecting the power of your positive thoughts puts you behind the wheel and keeps you from being victimized by events in your life. As a result, you live life from the inside out rather than from the outside in.

As a survivor of the Holocaust, psychiatrist Viktor Frankl came to understand a great deal about living life from the inside out. His closest family members were killed, he lost all his possessions, and he was imprisoned in a Nazi concentration camp. In spite of his suffering and his terrible losses, he declared his attitude could never be taken from him. He survived the unimaginable with a sense of hope. Fellow prisoners and even prison guards recognized that something was phenomenally different about this man and turned to him for help. In *Man's Search for Meaning*, he wrote about this experience:

> We who lived in concentration camps can remember the men who walked through the huts comforting others, giving away their last piece of bread. They may have been few in number, but they offer sufficient proof that everything can be taken from a man but one thing: the last of the human freedoms—

to choose one's attitude in any given set of circumstances, to choose one's own way.

Frankl's story illustrates the power of positive thinking amid the most horrific circumstances. Imagine the mastery it could give you over the challenges you face.

Positive thinking does not come naturally to everyone. People either tend toward optimism or pessimism. Whether we see the glass as half-full or half-empty depends on how we tend to explain to ourselves why events occur. While an optimist's approach discourages helplessness, Martin Seligman, the father of positive psychology, says a pessimist's mind-set fosters its development. According to Seligman, optimists share these characteristics:

- They tend to think a negative event is only a temporary setback.

- They tend to think the causes of a negative event are confined to that single case.

- They tend to think a negative event is not their fault. This does not mean they don't take responsibility for their actions. Rather, when something bad happens, optimists are less likely to view it is a result of their behavior.

- They catch relatively fewer infectious diseases, practice relatively better health habits, may have better immune systems, and are more likely to live longer.

In Seligman's view, the thinking of the pessimist presents a stark contrast:

- They tend to think a negative event is permanent. In their minds, circumstances don't change.

- They tend to think a negative event is pervasive, undermining everything they are trying to accomplish.

- They tend to think a negative event is a result of their own behavior. It is their fault.

- They will undermine whatever they do and, believing the problem will be permanent, are more likely than optimists to become depressed.

Depression is plaguing our society in epidemic numbers. In 2013, the incidence of depression was ten times more likely than fifty years ago, even allowing for a greater awareness of the illness. What's even more disconcerting is the increasing number of young people it affects. The average age of first onset fifty years ago was around thirty. Now it is below the age of fifteen. In my practice as a school psychologist, I have been astonished at the number of students under the age of twelve being treated for depression.

In addition, psychologists and psychiatrists are diagnosing unipolar and bipolar depression in young and old alike. Seligman defines *unipolar* as an exaggerated form of normal depression, calling it the "ultimate pessimism."

Most of us are familiar with the typical depression that results from the inevitable challenges and losses we experience. After a while, we bounce back. Clinical depression is different. It is a dark hole that seems inescapable, and it requires all of a sufferer's energy simply to put one foot in front of the other and go on living.

Depressives and nondepressives alike can share the characteristic of learned helplessness that leads to "the giving-up reaction." And, sometimes, this belief that whatever they do will not matter in a given situation contributes to a downward spiral into severe depression. Cognitive restructuring has proven to interrupt that plunge by teaching depressives to think more like optimists.

Though developing an optimistic mind-set is generally seen as a helpful tool in treating depression, Seligman cautions that unharnessed optimism can be dangerous and a degree of pessimism can keep us from becoming unrealistic. He endorses *flexible optimism*, which he describes as "optimism with its eyes open," an approach that prevents us from rushing into threatening or harmful situations.

ABC Management

The ABC model for cognitive restructuring developed by psychologist Albert Ellis looks like an algebra equation—A + B = C—and just like algebra, has real-life applications.

- A = the activating event

- B = your beliefs about it

- C = your consequential thoughts, feelings, and behaviors

To navigate life's ups and downs successfully, it's very important to keep B in the equation. If you aren't aware of the impact of your beliefs on your reaction to a given situation, cognitive restructuring can be very helpful. In other words, if your equation is A = C, you are failing to recognize the powerful impact of belief upon consequences. Consider the following A = C scenario:

A: You enter a neighborhood restaurant and encounter your neighbor, Nicole, whom you have not seen recently. You greet her with a smile and a cheerful "Hello." Nicole frowns and walks by you as if you were invisible.

C: You walk out of the restaurant without waiting to order your lunch, feeling hurt and rejected.

Employing the erroneous equation A = C, your feelings of rejection intensify as you walk down the street. Your thoughts might go something like this:

> *What just happened is not fair. I've been victimized by my neighbor with whom I just wanted to be friends. Nicole is a respected and influential person who is well-connected in our community. People are attracted to her. She has many wonderful friends. She does not like me. There must be something wrong with me. I just don't fit in here.*

All these spiraling thoughts are your beliefs—B—about the activating event A, and you have the power to change them before not after you react.

Remember the valid equation is A + B = C. The good news is that while there are many events in our lives over which we have little if any control, we do have control over B—the beliefs that we choose to adopt regarding such events. By restructuring our thoughts, we can influence the consequences C that we experience.

Let's see what happens when cognitive restructuring is applied to the B in the equation.

Following your encounter with Nicole, you think

> *Wow! That was odd. Nicole may have been preoccupied and unaware of my presence. She could be having a very stressful day. On the other hand, Nicole may have decided that she*

doesn't like me. Although I prefer to be liked, it's irrational to believe everyone is going to want to be my friend. Besides, whether or not she likes me does not change who I am. In fact, I'm the same person I was when I first walked in here.

Having taken charge of your beliefs about what just happened, the consequence—C—changes: *Although I feel somewhat perplexed following my encounter with Nicole, I will decide to follow up with a phone call later. For now I'm going to order my lunch as planned and enjoy myself.* That's the math that adds up to a positive frame of mind.

When we are able to control our beliefs about life events, we are empowered to create and maintain positive emotions, which have been proven to contribute a great deal to a sense of well-being and resilience in the face of stress. In fact, the research of social psychologist Barbara Fredrickson has found that the damage negative emotions have on the heart can be repaired by positive emotions. For example, unremitting stress, which is often accompanied by elevated heart rate, increased blood sugar, and suppression of the immune system, causes vulnerability to illness such as coronary disease. Experiencing positive emotions helps keep the body from becoming locked in that harmful chronic mode.

Examining how things go right rather than how they go wrong is the focus of Seligman's *positive psychology*. Many of its claims warrant our consideration. For instance, scientists have estimated that we remember only about one out of every one hundred pieces of information to which we are exposed. Our brains filter out information to avoid debilitating overload, retaining only the information deemed most pertinent. Like the spam blockers on our e-mail, only the most valued information is delivered to our memory banks.

In one experiment, subjects viewed a video of two basketball teams playing against each other. They were instructed to count the number of times the team wearing white shirts passed the ball. About twenty-five seconds after the video began, someone wearing a gorilla costume walked across the court right through the action, appearing on the screen for a full five seconds. After watching this video, the subjects were asked to write down the number of passes they counted. They were also asked if they had noticed anything unusual in the video.

Almost half of the two hundred people in the experiment totally missed the gorilla! Many of them were so amazed they didn't see something so obvious that they asked to view the video again.

Most of us tend to miss the gorilla in the room if that's not what we're looking for or expecting to find. In fact, we miss a lot, and if we have a pessimistic attitude, a lot of what we miss is the positive in life. Like science, the scriptures say we find what we are seeking (Matt. 7:7–8). How might our lives be different if our brains were continually seeking and intentionally focusing on the positive?

Consider the Choice: Do you tend to view the glass as half-full or as half-empty?

Count the Cost: Do the math. The valid equation is A + B = C. What are the benefits of considering your beliefs about an event before you react?

Claim the Promise: "Finally, brethren, whatsoever things are true, whatsoever things are honest, whatsoever things are just, whatsoever things are pure, whatsoever things are lovely, whatsoever things are of good report; if there be any virtue, and if there be any praise, think on these things . . . and the God of peace shall be with you" (Phil. 4:8–9). What promise do you glean from these scriptures?

Commit to the Cause: What can you do to ensure that you live your life intentionally, choosing to negate negative thinking?

Chapter 7

CHOOSE TO GIVE

"[R]emember the words of the Lord Jesus, how
he said, It is more blessed to give than to receive."
(Acts 20:35)

Tim Tebow may be as famous for the Bible-verse cita-
tions he paints on his face as he is for his quarterback-
ing. But multitudes apparently don't share his knowledge of
God's Word. After one championship game, he was amazed
to learn there were ninety-four million Google searches for
John 3:16. Many Christians, me included, count this beloved
passage among their first memorized scriptures: "For God
so loved the world, that he gave His only begotten Son. . . ."

Loving and Generous Lives

I might never have had the wonderful Christian upbringing I
did if it hadn't been for the generous spirit of a man from my
childhood known to me simply as J. D. Decades after it was
written, I found a copy of an old letter from J. D. dated April
16, 1958 in our family's safe deposit box—approximately

three months before my sixth birthday. He was an attorney writing to my birth mother, Norma:

> On March 4, 1958, I wrote you a letter relative to the desire of Mr. and Mrs. Gillespie to adopt Larry Russell Stacey. I have not been favored with any reply from you to this letter.
>
> I understand from Mrs. Gillespie that you now are not sure whether or not you would sign a consent to expedite this adoption. From what I understand, Mr. and Mrs. Gillespie have had this child virtually all of his life. . . . Consequently, I think it would be cruel and inhumane to Larry to ever take him from the Gillespies. It is with this premise in mind that I am writing you. . . .
>
> It seems to me that you once did what was best for Larry when you let him live with the Gillespies. At this time you apparently put Larry first. Now, when you are asked to put Larry first again, you find it difficult because you think you are giving something away which belongs to you. Actually, I feel that you are giving Larry something which belongs to him. . . . The Gillespies love Larry and apparently Larry loves them as if they were his natural parents. . . .
>
> Larry has a right to belong to the Gillespies and to have the Gillespies belong to him. This is all that you are being asked

to do now, and that is to consummate in the eyes of the law a matter which has already been consummated in Larry's eyes and the eyes of the Lord. . . . I do think it is to Larry's best interest and personally beg you to give every consideration to Larry's rights in this matter, for if you put Larry first, you can do nothing but sign a consent for his adoption and expedite the matter in every way possible. . . .

Mrs. Gillespie was my birth mother's older sister, Ruby, who was happily married to Buck. Norma was a single mother, and during the 1950s, such a life was difficult indeed. The sisters loved each other deeply, but their lives had taken radically different trajectories. Thanks to J. D., my birth mother chose to do the right thing.

The adoption was finalized the following December. I remain eternally grateful for J. D.'s gift of influence. I believe that he allowed God to advocate for me through him when I could not defend myself. My gratitude extends to Norma for her courage to give me the family I needed and to my heavenly Father for this and countless other favors extended to me throughout my life. I feel like I have been granted the privilege of riding His wave. As a result, I am compelled to give to others in the manner that God sees fit: "For unto whomsoever much is given, of him shall be much required. . . ." (Luke 12:48). As my blessings have mounted over the years, this passage of scripture has become increasingly meaningful to me.

Momma and Poppa modeled the scriptures of gratitude and generosity in public and at home. When I needed a mother and father, they unselfishly stepped up. They grieved over the loss of their own two baby boys but refused to become bitter. Instead, they seized the opportunity to adopt me, choosing to view this as a blessing from God.

They fell in love with each other at an early age and later fell in love with God. They saw themselves as God saw them and loved others with an authentic love that was contagious. From them, I learned that it is possible to give without loving but impossible to love without giving. I saw them embrace others in their hearts, as well as their arms, regardless of race, color, creed, or station in life. They gave of their time, talents, material goods, prayers, and spiritual wisdom, and they graciously and gratefully received the gifts of others. So you see, Ruby and Buck modeled the COPING Strategy long before I ever thought of trying to define it. For that, I am eternally grateful.

The Love Principle modeled by my parents is at the heart of Christianity, and over the past few decades, its message of generosity—spiritual and material—has become a topic of research and conversation far beyond the church. Scientists are actually studying the effects of generosity on individuals and society. Bioethicist Dr. Stephen Post heads up the Institute for Research on Unlimited Love. In *Why Good Things Happen to Good People*, he and co-author Jill Neimark describe giving as being "the most potent force on the planet," one that "you can always choose" and "will protect you your whole life long."

The headline-making studies Post conducts provide ample evidence of the benefits of living a loving and generous life. The scientists of a British think tank agree. One of their reports associates enhanced well-being and prevention of mental illness with "giving to neighbors and communities."

Scores of studies indicate that when we choose to give of ourselves, we are happier and healthier, live longer, and enjoy a greater sense of well-being and prosperity. Post and Neimark elaborate on numerous ways of giving that yield such benefits. Examples include sending thank-you notes, returning calls, sharing wisdom and knowledge, extending forgiveness, sharing a sense of humor, accepting people unconditionally, sympathizing with others, being dependable, etc.

You can no doubt think of many other ways to give constructively to others and welcome what others do for you. My friend Martha, for instance, wanted to leave a meaningful legacy for her grandchildren. After praying and waiting for an answer, she decided to leave them "passwords." During her private time with each of her grandchildren, she teaches them Bible verses—passwords—to a life of Christian faith: "It is more blessed to give than to receive" (Acts 20:35) and "I can do all things through Christ which strengtheneth me" (Phil. 4:13) are examples, among many others. Martha's grandchildren are getting a head start on timeless truths that will enhance their lives both in this world and the one to come because their grandmother thought of this unique, creative gift.

Nine Ways to Be Nice

There is plenty of research that supports the benefits of altruistic behavior—not that we need scientists to tell us to be kind. Just look around. You'll see that people living happy, successful lives tend to make giving a habit. My wife, Diane, and I created a way of giving we call "Nine Ways to Be Nice." We simply challenge each other to seize at least nine opportunities to be kind every day. After many years, I can't even count all the acts of kindness, large or small. Here are just a few:

- Saying "I love you" to each other

- Hugging a friend

- Visiting a shut-in

- Baking a "welcome cake" for new neighbors

- Contributing care, time, or monetary support for friends in need

- Removing grocery carts from a parking lot

- Carrying an elderly lady's luggage at the airport

- Having friends over for dinner

- Giving copies of *The COPING Strategy* to those who express an interest

I don't list these acts as badges to be worn for commendation. This sort of behavior should be typical rather than exceptional, particularly among those of us who are Christ's followers. The Bible says, "[F]or whatsoever a man soweth, that shall he also reap" (Gal. 6:7). Over the years, Diane and I have reaped the many benefits of giving and have been able to help and encourage others along the way. We remain mindful of the admonition of Jesus: "Take heed that ye do not your alms before men, to be seen of them: otherwise ye have no reward of your Father which is in heaven" (Matt. 6:1).

We can all agree that generosity is a good thing, but it has to be constructive. Most of us have someone in our lives to whom we could give everything, right down to the shirts off our backs, and they would behave irresponsibly with our gifts. "Give a man a fish and he eats for a day; teach a man to fish and he eats for a lifetime," says the truism. Sometimes, it's appropriate to do both. Always return to the critical question: "If I do this, is it going to help?"

In order to give constructively, we must ensure we don't place others or ourselves in danger. Unfortunately, it isn't always safe to be kind. For example, though I would love to help a hitchhiker sticking out his thumb in the rain, I don't. Picking up a stranger could put my family and me at risk. I also try to remain mindful that it is often irresponsible for me to offer money to the panhandlers holding up their signs on the median strips: "Hungry. Please help." Some might be truly hungry, but others are collecting money for alcohol or drugs, and still others consider this an appropriate way to make a meager living. Consider constructive alternatives to giving cash, like dropping off a sack lunch or a card with the name of the nearest food bank or shelter. Of course, it's always a good idea to donate to reputable outreach organizations for the homeless and destitute. Supporting an organization that gives to the needy is a very constructive way to be kind *and* safe.

The Fundamental People Skill

Loving authentically and giving to others responsibly requires the fundamental people skill *empathy*, which is the ability to accurately perceive someone else's feelings and understand their condition from their perspective.

Early in my career as a counselor, a little girl taught me much of what I need to know about empathy. I witnessed her interaction with a paraprofessional in a school in which I was working. The girl said she was not feeling well and described her symptoms in great detail. The kind lady listened with genuine interest and told her she had recently felt much the same way. Subsequently, the two came up with a plan that might help. Later in the day, I was alone in the front office when the same little girl approached the reception desk.

"Can I help you?" I asked kindly, wanting to put her at ease.

She looked me over and responded, "I don't think so. Where's that lady who understands exactly how I feel?"

That's the power of empathy!

Our capacity to empathize begins in our immediate relationships and builds with involvement in friendships, the workplace, teams, communities, and beyond. It is something that is instilled through modeling, mentoring, coaching, and storytelling, which have proven to be powerful vehicles for teaching and developing empathy.

Empathy is nurtured by *active listening*, which is listening to not just words but the feelings behind them without making judgments. The psychoanalyst Theodor Reik called it "listening with the third ear." Active listening may require separating the person from their behavior. That way, you can communicate genuine caring without condoning behavior you don't agree with. For instance, you might be unaccepting of your friend's drug addiction, while accepting him unconditionally as your friend.

The feedback you offer as a result of active listening isn't all verbal. Eye contact, nodding, and facial and body expressions, as well as your words, reassure the other person that you have not only heard but understand. Responses like these communicate that you know how the other person feels:

> I hear you saying . . .
> It sounds as if . . .
> So you are saying . . .
> It's sort of like . . .

The Note from Linda

Do you recall the note I received from a stranger three days before Momma died? "Hang in there," it said. "Remember: There is no decision you have to make that God doesn't feel you can handle. Peace to you."

She signed the note "Linda." I assumed her act of kindness would otherwise remain anonymous, and it would have, except for the fact that God works in mysterious ways.

In the early 1990s, my father and I boarded a packed flight in Houston. Poppa was seated on the aisle. I was seated next to him in the middle seat, and the window seat remained vacant. At the last minute, a harried but pleasant-looking lady pointed to the vacant window seat.

"I believe that's mine," she said. Then she turned and looked at me. "Have we met?" she asked. Then her eyes widened. "Baptist Hospital!"

The mysterious lady with the note reappeared in my life! After all those years, under the most unlikely circumstances, Linda and I had the perfect opportunity to talk and get to know each other. What are the chances of that?

I told her how meaningful her note had been to me and countless others with whom I had shared it. Before the end of the flight, I got the chance to share a kindness in return.

Linda had just visited with her sister, who was going through a difficult divorce. She told me how much she grieved for her sister's distress. I took out a piece of paper and printed the word "COPING" and a summary of the six keys in the COPING Strategy. The principle of reciprocity went full circle as she accepted my heart's passion in gratitude for the powerful message she had given to me.

I believe that God uses ordinary people like you, me, and Linda to deliver His mail. I am thankful that she chose to invest all of perhaps five minutes in me, a distressed stranger with whom she empathized. Expecting nothing in return, she simply decided to contribute something that would help me through my mother's last hours. She knew that we both shared the same human condition and that we are both dependent upon a power that transcends ourselves.

After my mother died, I put Linda's note away for safekeeping in a place so secure that, over the years, not even I could find it. But that was not the end of it. Linda's message was destined to impact me once again.

In May 2008, Diane and I had just closed on the sale of our house. Our new neighbors were throwing a party to welcome us and tell their old neighbors goodbye. That night, instead of going to the party, I was in the emergency room at Baptist Hospital.

I was soon diagnosed with colon cancer.

Diane and I were numb. It was as if we'd been enjoying a perfect day at the beach when we got knocked down by a huge wave we didn't see coming. In an instant, the whole world changed for us. Even with our deep faith, the "C" word was huge. Just saying it proved difficult. Although we both knew that God was going to continue to take care of us, we were scared, and we grieved.

Before my scheduled surgery, I was cleaning out the garage, anticipating our upcoming move when I came across a little box. Inside was Linda's note. Almost two decades after its initial appearance, her message ministered in a powerful way to Diane and me. It reminded us that God was watching over us and that with His help, we would cope with our uncertain future.

The Best Gift

Initially, we did not know my prognosis. We prayed for God's favor, uniting our faith with the faith of others. I am grateful for the many friends and strangers who prayed and gave so freely of themselves during that time. One group gifted us with a prayer shawl they made for me to use when I was taking my chemotherapy. It is proudly draped over the back of a chair in my study. Just looking at it gives me strength to this day. Others sent cards and e-mails assuring us of their prayers on my behalf. Our experience confirmed the utter necessity of the human connection. I can't overstate the tremendous healing quality that came with the knowledge that others recognized the significance of what we were experiencing and genuinely cared.

I continue to ask God to favor and bless all of those who gave so unselfishly of themselves during our time of treatment and recovery. They are continual reminders to me that a genuinely empathetic heart is one of the greatest gifts we can give.

While no one would likely volunteer for this journey, Diane and I ended up in places we otherwise would never have gone and met people we would never have met. We are grateful for those encounters and the opportunities we have been given to reciprocate the acts of kindness, sometimes in unexpected ways.

One of my nurses at the hospital, an attractive young woman, had commendable clinical skills, but she was guarded and kept conversation to a minimum. Though she provided care for me day after day, she maintained her distance for some time. One day, she looked at me and said, "You have a peace about you. I've known a few people who have had that kind of peace, and I've thought that some day I would like to have that kind of peace too." That was quite a mouthful from someone who had spoken little to me since my admission.

Diane and I were delighted to share the source of that peace with her. She prayed with us on several occasions and revealed a compassionate heart beneath that rather cool demeanor. She said she would like her two little girls to experience the peace that we talked about, and I suggested the best way for them to experience it was for her to model it. "After work, I'm going to go home and get my Bible out," she said. I felt honored to have the opportunity to witness for God's divine love, the source of all peace.

The nurse was right. I did experience a sense of peace at one of the most significant crossroads in my life. I believe it was a gift from a power that transcends me. I can't analyze or define it, but I have experienced that gift, and I have found its revelation in the sacred writings of the Holy Scriptures. As a result of that revelation, I have nurtured a relationship with its source.

The best gift that I could possibly give to you would be an introduction to this source.

> **Consider the Choice**: You can choose to isolate yourself from the human community, or you can choose to join it, knowing that by doing so, you become a part of the healing circle of giving.

Count the Cost: How many acts of kindness are you willing to perform each day? Which option are you willing to embrace?

Claim the Promise: What promise do you glean from the following scripture passage? "Give, and it shall be given unto you; good measure, pressed down, and shaken together, and running over, shall men give into your bosom. For with the same measure that ye mete withal it shall be measured to you again" (Luke 6:38).

Commit to the Cause: Recognize the healing power of giving. Choose to give to others and allow others to give to you in a manner that is responsible.

Chapter 8

MAINTAINING THE COPING STRATEGY

"This is a faithful saying, and these things I will
that thou affirm constantly, that they which have
believed in God might be careful to maintain good
works. These things are good and profitable unto
men." (Titus 3:8)

The critical final step required in order to successfully implement the COPING Strategy came to me after watching school maintenance teams repaint wood trim, replace sagging gutters, and change out filters on heating systems. In the three-plus decades I worked for the school board, I gained knowledge from many colleagues, students, and parents, but after watching the maintenance department in action, I realized the Strategy could not succeed if I failed to stress the necessity of its regular maintenance.

They fixed leaking roofs, clogged plumbing, and broken heaters, but much more of their energy went into installing new roofs before they began to leak, replacing worn pipes so they would not break, and painting wood so it would not rot. Their primary job was preventive.

It's no different for us. We all need a personal maintenance department, and, like the team taking care of the school buildings where I worked, it has to focus on prevention. You can choose to spend your time and energy putting out one fire after another, plugging up leaks, fixing the fence with baling wire, or you can work on preventing crises from happening in the first place.

Your Personal Maintenance Plan

- Choose each day to maintain control from the inside out.

- Choose each day to maintain a strong and realistic sense of self-efficacy married to character.

- Choose each day to maintain a relationship with God that gives meaning and purpose to a self-transcendent life.

- Choose each day to maintain personal initiative.

- Choose each day to maintain a sense of optimism with your eyes wide open.

- Choose each day to maintain a heart of gratitude and generosity.

This is the essence of the six key points of the COPING Strategy, but reading about them is not enough. The

COPING Strategy is not a one-time gig. It has to be executed regularly and with intention. This plan will keep the Strategy alive in your life. Over time, the virtues and principles will become an indelible part of your character, and the choices you make will increase your quality of life in this world and the one yet to come. Here are a few ideas for executing the maintenance plan in your life:

- Incorporate the COPING Strategy into your personal devotion time. Ask God to help you implement each of the six principles of the Strategy daily, stating each of them specifically. Thank Him for the truths these principles are based upon and the benefits you are experiencing.

- Keep a copy of *The COPING Strategy* prominently displayed and review it often.

- Share the Strategy. We all deal with the wear and tear of daily life. If you share the Strategy in a non-judgmental manner, it will bring welcome relief. Sharing the Strategy also provides a non-intrusive way of presenting the Christian faith. Consider leading a COPING Strategy study group at church, work, or elsewhere in your community.

- Develop your personal mission statement and review it often.

- Practice Nine Ways to Be Nice.

- Refer to the Sources/References in *The COPING Strategy* and learn more from the many works I consulted.

- Keep a journal. Record the benefits you experience as a result of implementing the Strategy and review them regularly.

- Review your Personal Maintenance Plan often and gauge your progress.

Develop the Habit of COPING

Devoting yourself to the COPING Strategy is a *keystone habit*. It has the potential to have a major impact, initiating a process, that when practiced consistently, transforms everything else. A keystone habit gets the ball rolling, and other patterns in your life will change in its wake.

New York Times investigative reporter Charles Duhigg coined the term keystone habit. In his research for *The Power of Habit: Why We Do What We Do*, he discovered that when individuals begin to exercise habitually, they also begin to change other patterns in their lives, often without conscious awareness. They frequently start eating better, become more productive, are more patient, smoke less, use their credit cards less frequently, and report that they feel less stressed. Exercise makes other desirable habits easier to put into practice.

Identifying keystone habits can be challenging. We have to know where to look. What better place than in the wisdom of the sacred writings? Practiced consistently, they infuse everything they touch with their goodness. Reviewing the six keys of the COPING Strategy on a regular basis can begin the journey toward this end.

My way of making sure the six keys remain at the front of my mind is to incorporate the COPING Strategy into my daily devotions. It is a wonderful way to start the day. After expressing my thankfulness for God's blessings, I prayerfully ask Him for his support:

- Help me choose to compensate constructively.

- Help me choose to overcome.

- Help me choose to pause in order to provide time for nurturing my spirit.

- Help me choose to initiate.

- Help me choose to negate negative thinking.

- Help me choose to give of myself to others and allow others to give to me in a manner that is responsible.

I conclude my prayers by acknowledging that all of the glory for all that is good belongs to Him.

The COPING Strategy has been a habit of mine for decades. Consequently, these six keystones have permeated my life. These choices reflect how I view everything. They are my mission. They represent who I want to be.

I am an earthen vessel, far from perfect and prone to mistakes. But my keystone habits help keep me anchored in a broken world. When I follow their direction, they serve me exceedingly well. When I have yielded to contrary winds, it has been to my peril. They are like friends who always have my back, protecting and providing for me.

Saint Paul has a soothing prayer for us, God's earthen vessels: "And the very God of peace sanctify you wholly; and I pray God your whole spirit and soul and body be preserved blameless unto the coming of our Lord Jesus Christ" (1 Thess. 5:23). You are a spirit who has a soul that lives in a body. These aspects of you are so intimately interwoven. It is difficult to define where one ends and another begins. When any one of these aspects of your being is not well, the others are negatively impacted, and you are not whole.

Body, soul, and spirit all need regular maintenance. Care for your body by choosing to exercise regularly, get enough rest, eat a well-balanced diet, seek medical care when it is required, and avoid high-risk behaviors. Care for your soul by choosing to manage your emotions effectively, monitor your thinking, and make constructive decisions. Beyond body and soul, we are spirit. Our spirits constitute our core beings that long to find meaning and purpose in our lives. Our spirits reach Godward and ultimately find wholeness in Him. Care for your spirit by choosing to nurture and support your journey toward God and your connection with Him.

Living in wholeness with God means following His law. The aim of the COPING Strategy is to share the keys to this way of life. George Washington spoke eloquently about this strategy for success over two hundred years ago in his first inaugural address: "The propitious smiles of Heaven can never be expected on a nation that disregards the eternal rules of order and right which Heaven itself hath ordained." The message was straightforward. If our new nation were to attract the divine favor and blessings of God, its people would have to play by God's rules.

All power belongs to God, and He chooses to place His power in us. The choices woven into the tapestries of our lives must be driven by our submission to Him and the revelation that we have of Him in the Holy Scriptures. Then and only then, shall His divine will be fulfilled in our lives. Indeed, "the conclusion of the whole matter" is to "Fear God, and keep his commandments: for this is the whole duty of man" (Eccles. 12:13).

I have prayed for you to become marked as a target that will continually attract the favor and blessings of Our Gracious, Loving, Heavenly Father. Let the fulfillment begin!

Chapter 9

BEYOND THE COPING STRATEGY

"Trust in the LORD with all thine heart; and lean
not unto thine own understanding. In all thy ways
acknowledge him, and he shall direct thy paths."
(Prov. 3:5-6)

The COPING Strategy is the result of a lifetime of studying the wisdom of the scriptures, psychology, and related
disciplines, as well as personal experience negotiating the
challenges that accompany living in a broken world. The
Strategy was inspired by countless individuals whose paths
crossed mine and whose stories enlightened me, but one
who has taught me much about walking in God's path has
been my wife Diane.

After Diane's husband, Bert, died in a tragic accident,
she grieved deeply. Though she was surrounded by sup-
portive friends and anchored in her Christian faith, she was
hurting as she had never hurt before. In the hours following
Bert's sudden death, Diane's world was spinning. Seeking to

regain some sense of control, she retreated to her closet for a private audience with God.

Diane was angry. She told God that she could not go on living without Bert.

Then something phenomenal happened. Diane heard a voice, loud and clear: "I am the only one you can't live without."

And so, her healing began.

Diane is a remarkable lady. Like the rest of us, she is not perfect. She experienced a period in her early adulthood when she strayed from the faith instilled in her by her parents, but she renewed her commitment to that faith.

When Bert first asked her out, she told him she wouldn't date him unless he went to church with her. Bert renewed his faith and personal relationship with God and began sharing the Good News, teaching Sunday School at church and a Bible study at work. He had already prepared the lesson for the next Sunday when he accidentally drowned in the backyard pool. Ironically, the title of that lesson was "The Value of Human Life."

Bert's renewed commitment to his faith contributed immeasurably to Diane's healing after his death. She is confident that his faith made him a recipient of eternal life with God. From her perspective, Christians do not die. "They just get transfers!" she says. She and I have visited his grave in the country cemetery in South Georgia, but she does not think of the stone as marking his grave. Rather, it designates his "resurrection spot." This type of reframing has been helpful to Diane in dealing with her significant loss.

There are other keys of the COPING Strategy that Diane chose to further her emotional healing. For instance, through her close connection to God, she found meaning and purpose in her loss, and she has chosen not to waste her pain. She is gifted in her ability to minister loving care to her patients and coworkers, as well as their loved ones, at the hospital where she works. Her loss has birthed a deep level of empathy and given her credibility with people who are hurting. This is post-traumatic growth.

Diane chose to respond to her loss by becoming better rather than bitter. She recognized that life is about choices—some choices advance us toward growth and wholeness, while others result in regression and brokenness.

Diane's wonderful care helped carry me through one of the most difficult challenges I ever faced. The cancer that invaded my body demanded an all-out response on all levels—physical, emotional, and spiritual—and Diane was with me every step of the way.

The chemotherapy went on for months. My fellow sufferers and I spent hours side by side in recliners at the oncologist's office, letting the toxic drugs flow into our veins. They sent me home with a pump strapped to my side that continued to propel chemicals into my body.

After twenty-four hours, I returned to the doctor's office and repeated the same routine. On Wednesdays, I returned home without the pump, but I reported to my doctor's office on Thursday for an injection. After that, I got a reprieve until a week from the following Monday. This was the general routine all that summer and fall.

Those of us receiving treatments were all weakened by disease, as well as by the poison being pumped into our bodies, but many of us did not hesitate to introduce ourselves and share our stories. We were all in the same boat to some extent, and this made it easy to connect. Each of us knew much about how the others felt. This was truly empathy in action. From our separate recliners with plastic containers holding our respective medications hanging above us, we often shared quick smiles and genuine words of encouragement, including the strength that a number of us were drawing from our faith.

I also remember the somber looks and soft whispers when an empty recliner broadcast the dreaded news that one of our company had lost the battle. We grieved for their families and friends, and we grieved for ourselves. Such news confronted us with our own mortality. At the same time, it galvanized our resolve to fight the dreaded disease that ravaged our bodies. The empty recliner prompted me to spend more time counting my blessings and practicing the art of gratitude. I thanked God for the privilege of remaining among the living.

I wrestled with survivor's guilt. Indeed, years later, at times I still do. Why did I remain when so many others, like the young mother of teenagers, did not?

I came to realize the disease that had taken its toll was a result of living in a broken world contaminated by sin. I also recognized that through my relationship with God, I could take the most dreadful and seemingly unfair situation and birth meaning and purpose from it. I chose to immerse myself in God's grace as I healed. And I thanked God even more than before for the gift of Diane.

I had irresponsibly postponed a colonoscopy on numerous occasions for several years. I rationalized my procrastination, thinking I was too busy, promising myself I would schedule it later. When my symptoms appeared, Diane insisted that I go to the hospital for the procedure that proved critical to saving my life. A colonoscopy revealed a tumor in my colon.

I was admitted to the hospital for surgery, and Diane remained with me day and night until I was discharged. Over the following months, she accompanied me to all of my chemo sessions and doctor appointments. With her at my side, I had the best around-the-clock nursing care imaginable.

Motivated by her profound love for me, Diane searched for ways to help me when the disease presented formidable challenges. She found practical things that made huge differences. She discovered that I would eat blueberry muffins when I did not have an appetite for anything else. So we ate more blueberry muffins than I can count. When the chemo caused severe nerve damage, she massaged my hands and feet to ease the pain. When the condition made my feet feel like they were frozen, she ordered small electric blankets to wrap them and beanbag slippers she warmed in the microwave. The warmth brought wonderful relief. By now, you can see I am undeniably spoiled.

I am also most undoubtedly blessed.

Diane loves me, but most importantly, she loves God. She has a personal and intimate relationship with Him. Many times, she has smiled at me and declared, "Jesus loves you, but I'm His favorite!" Her faith runs deep, and she talks with Him often. This is how she lives her life.

There were nights when I was weaker than I can find words to describe. In the early hours before dawn, I would awaken and feel Diane's gentle hand on my back. I knew what she was doing. She was asking God for favor for me, and she believed wholeheartedly that her request would be granted. How do you quantify the value of that?

One afternoon, the oncologist called and informed us the cancer had spread to my liver. He said another surgery was inevitable and recommended we schedule an appointment with a surgeon. Diane and I were disappointed and afraid, but we agreed that "these are the sorts of situations where God likes to show up."

I believed God would take care of me, and if that meant having the second surgery, I would entrust myself to Him. But we didn't believe that the surgery was inevitable. We turned once again to prayer, asking God for favor, making the second surgery unnecessary. I am humbled by the number of friends who prayed for me, and I am thankful.

Weeks later, I got a phone call from my oncologist. Examining the latest scans, the radiologists could not find the spot on my liver. What's more, after prolonged study of the scans, my astounded oncologist was unable to document any indication of the disease.

Not only did I not need surgery, but my oncologist also discontinued my chemo sessions. Diane and I got this good news during the Christmas season. We had much to celebrate. The favor we had petitioned for in our prayers had been granted. Our tests had now become our testimonies.

Including Diane in my prayers and being included in her prayers has been a blessing for me. She tells me she prays for me more than she prays for herself, and I am humbled. She is indeed a gift from God.

In addition to sharing the COPING Strategy with you, I am encouraging you to love God as Diane does, forging an intimate connection that will guide you through the challenges still to come. I believe this choice will determine your eternal destiny. It is the most important decision you will ever make.

I invite you to ask God to establish His kingdom within your heart if you have not already done so (See Appendix C). Accept His invitation to come into your heart. Believe He died to pay for your sins. Confess you have sinned and desire His forgiveness. This will establish a divine relationship according to His Word. Abide in His love and maintain this relationship eternally.

Congratulations! You now have God's grace and the tools of the COPING Strategy supporting you in every challenge you face. Celebrate and look forward to experiencing a whole life in the midst of a broken world!

APPENDIX A

THE COPING STRATEGY

Accompanying Scripture References from the King
James Version of the Holy Bible

Choose to Compensate Constructively

Deuteronomy 30:19

I call heaven and earth to record this day against you, that I have set before you life and death, blessing and cursing: therefore choose life, that both thou and thy seed may live . . .

Joshua 24:15

And if it seem evil unto you to serve the Lord, choose you this day, whom ye will serve; whether the gods which your fathers served that were on the other side of the flood, or the gods of the Amorites, in whose land ye dwell: but as for me and my house, we will serve the Lord.

Psalm 119:173

Let thine hand help me; for I have chosen thy precepts.

Proverbs 3:5–6

Trust in the Lord with all thine heart; and lean not unto thine own understanding. In all thy ways acknowledge him, and he shall direct thy paths.

Jeremiah 6:16

Thus saith the Lord, Stand ye in the ways, and see, and ask for the old paths, where is the good way, and walk therein, and ye shall find rest for your souls. But they said, We will not walk therein.

Haggai 1:5–7

Now therefore thus saith the LORD of hosts; Consider your ways. Ye have sown much, and bring in little; ye eat, but ye have not enough; ye drink, but ye are not filled with drink; ye clothe you, but there is none warm; and he that earneth wages earneth wages to put it into a bag with holes. Thus saith the LORD of hosts; Consider your ways.

Matthew 6:21

For where your treasure is, there will your heart be also.

Matthew 22:35–40

Then one of them, which was a lawyer, asked him a question, tempting him, and saying, Master, which is the great commandment in the law? Jesus said unto him, Thou shalt love the Lord thy God with all thy heart, and with all thy soul, and with all thy mind. This is the first and great commandment. And the second is like unto it, Thou shalt love thy neighbor as thyself. On these two commandments hang all the law and the prophets.

John 13:34

A new commandment I give unto you, That ye love one another; as I have loved you, that ye also love one another.

Galatians 5:14

For all the law is fulfilled in one word, even in this; Thou shalt love thy neighbor as thyself.

Colossians 3:14

And above all these things put on charity, which is the bond of perfectness.

Hebrews 11:24-25

By faith Moses, when he was come to years, refused to be called the son of Pharaoh's daughter; Choosing rather to suffer affliction with the people of God, than to enjoy the pleasures of sin for a season . . .

Choose to Overcome

Numbers 13:30, 31, & 33

And Caleb stilled the people before Moses, and said, Let us go up at once, and possess it; for we are well able to overcome it. But the men that went up with him said, We be not able to go up against the people; for they are stronger than we . . . And there we saw the giants, the sons of Anak, which come of the giants: and we were in our own sight as grasshoppers, and so we were in their sight.

Psalm 8:3–6

When I consider thy heavens, the work of thy fingers, the moon and the stars, which thou hast ordained; What is man, that thou art mindful of him? and the son of man, that thou visitest him? For thou hast made him a little lower than the angels, and hast crowned him with glory and honour. Thou madest him to have dominion over the works of thy hands . . .

Isaiah 54:17

No weapon that is formed against thee shall prosper. . . .

Romans 8:37

Nay, in all these things we are more than conquerors through him that loved us.

Romans 12:3–5

For I say, through the grace given unto me, to every man that is among you, not to think of himself more highly than he ought to think; but to think soberly, according as God hath dealt to every man the measure of faith. For as we have many members in one body, and all members have not the same office: So we, being many, are one body in Christ, and every one members one of another.

Romans 12:21

Be not overcome of evil, but overcome evil with good.

2 Corinthians 3:4–5

And such trust have we through Christ to God-ward: Not that we are sufficient of ourselves to think any thing as of ourselves; but our sufficiency is of God . . .

2 Corinthians 12:9–10

And he said unto me, My grace is sufficient for thee: for my strength is made perfect in weakness. Most gladly therefore will I rather glory in my infirmities, that the power of Christ may rest upon me. Therefore I take pleasure in infirmities, in reproaches, in necessities, in persecutions, in distresses for Christ's sake: for when I am weak, then am I strong.

Galatians 6:9

And let us not be weary in well doing: for in due season we shall reap, if we faint not.

Philippians 4:13

I can do all things through Christ which strengtheneth me.

1 John 4:4

Ye are of God, little children, and have overcome them: because greater is he that is in you, than he that is in the world.

Revelation 2:7

To him that overcometh will I give to eat of the tree of life, which is in the midst of the paradise of God.

Revelation 2:11

He that overcometh shall not be hurt of the second death.

Revelation 2:26

And he that overcometh, and keepeth my works unto the end, to him will I give power over the nations . . .

Revelation 3:5

He that overcometh, the same shall be clothed in white raiment; and I will not blot out his name out of the book of life, but I will confess his name before my Father, and before his angels.

Revelation 3:12

Him that overcometh will I make a pillar in the temple of my God, and he shall go no more out: and I will write upon him the name of my God, and the name of the city of my God, which is new Jerusalem, which cometh down out of heaven from my God: and I will write upon him my new name.

Revelation 12:11

And they overcame him by the blood of the Lamb, and by the word of their testimony. . . .

Revelation 21:7

He that overcometh shall inherit all things; and I will be his God, and he shall be my son.

Choose to Pause to Nurture Your Spirit

Deuteronomy 8:18

But thou shalt remember the Lord thy God: for it is he that giveth thee power to get wealth, that he may establish his covenant which he sware unto thy fathers, as it is this day.

Joshua 1:8

This book of the law shall not depart out of thy mouth; but thou shalt meditate therein day and night, that thou mayest observe to do according to all that is written therein: for then thou shalt make thy way prosperous, and then thou shalt have good success.

Nehemiah 8:10

[F]or the joy of the LORD is your strength.

Psalm 1:1–3

Blessed is the man that walketh not in the counsel of the ungodly, nor standeth in the way of sinners, nor sitteth in the seat of the scornful. But his delight is in the law of the Lord; and in his law doeth he meditate day and night. And he shall be like a tree planted by the rivers of water, that bringeth forth his fruit in his season; his leaf also shall not wither; and whatsoever he doeth shall prosper.

Psalm 19:14

Let the words of my mouth, and the meditation of my heart, be acceptable in thy sight, O LORD, my strength, and my redeemer.

Psalm 46:10

Be still, and know that I am God. . . .

Psalm 62:11–12

God hath spoken once; twice have I heard this; that power belongeth unto God. Also unto thee, O Lord, belongeth mercy: for thou renderest to every man according to his work.

Psalm 119:165

Great peace have they which love thy law: and nothing shall offend them.

Psalm 138:8

The LORD will perfect that which concerneth me: thy mercy, O LORD, endureth forever: forsake not the works of thine own hands.

Proverbs 17:1

Better is a dry morsel, and quietness therewith, than an house full of sacrifices with strife.

Isaiah 32:18

And my people shall dwell in a peaceable habitation, and in sure dwellings, and in quiet resting places . . .

Matthew 7:7–8

Ask, and it shall be given you; seek, and ye shall find; knock, and it shall be opened unto you: For every one that asketh receiveth; and he that seeketh findeth; and to him that knocketh it shall be opened.

Matthew 22:34–40

But when the Pharisees had heard that he had put the Sadducees to silence, they were gathered together. Then one of them, which was a lawyer, asked him a question, tempting him, and saying, Master, which is the great commandment in the law? Jesus said unto him, Thou shalt love the Lord thy God with all thy heart, and with all thy soul, and with all thy mind. This is the first and great commandment. And the second is like unto it, Thou shalt love thy neighbor as thyself. On these two commandments hang all the law and the prophets.

Matthew 28:18–20

And Jesus came and spake unto them, saying, All power is given unto me in heaven and in earth. Go ye therefore, and teach all nations, baptizing them in the name of the Father, and of the Son, and of the Holy Ghost: Teaching them to observe all things whatsoever I have commanded you: and, lo, I am with you alway, even unto the end of the world. Amen.

John 10:10–11

The thief cometh not, but for to steal, and to kill, and to destroy: I am come that they might have life, and that they might have it more abundantly. I am the good shepherd: the good shepherd giveth his life for the sheep.

John 15:7

If ye abide in me, and my words abide in you, ye shall ask what ye will, and it shall be done unto you.

John 16:23–24

Whatsoever ye shall ask the Father in my name, he will give it you. Hitherto have ye asked nothing in my name: ask, and ye shall receive, that your joy may be full.

Romans 8:28

And we know that all things work together for good to them that love God, to them who are the called according to his purpose.

Galatians 5:22–23

But the fruit of the Spirit is love, joy, peace, longsuffering, gentleness, goodness, faith, Meekness, temperance: against such there is no law.

Ephesians 2:10

For we are his workmanship, created in Christ Jesus unto good works, which God hath before ordained that we should walk in them.

Philippians 4:6–7

Be careful for nothing; but in every thing by prayer and supplication with thanksgiving let your requests be made known unto God. And the peace of God, which passeth all understanding, shall keep your hearts and minds through Christ Jesus.

Colossians 3:14

And above all these things put on charity, which is the bond of perfectness.

1 Thessalonians 4:11

[S]tudy to be quiet . . .

1 Thessalonians 5:17–18

Pray without ceasing. In every thing give thanks: for this is the will of God in Christ Jesus concerning you.

2 Timothy 3:16

All scripture is given by inspiration of God, and is profitable for doctrine, for reproof, for correction, for instruction in righteousness . . .

Hebrews 4:12

For the word of God is quick, and powerful, and sharper than any twoedged sword, piercing even to the dividing asunder of soul and spirit, and of the joints and marrow, and is a discerner of the thoughts and intents of the heart.

Hebrews 4:14–16

Seeing then that we have a great high priest, that is passed into the heavens, Jesus the Son of God, let us hold fast our profession. For we have not an high priest which cannot be touched with the feeling of our infirmities; but was in all points tempted like as we are, yet without sin. Let us therefore come boldly unto the throne of grace, that we may obtain mercy, and find grace to help in time of need.

James 1:2-3

My brethren, count it all joy when ye fall into divers temptations; Knowing this, that the trying of your faith worketh patience.

James 4:2-3

Ye lust, and have not: ye kill, and desire to have, and cannot obtain: ye fight and war, yet ye have not, because ye ask not. Ye ask, and receive not, because ye ask amiss, that ye may consume it upon your lusts.

Choose to Initiate

Genesis 1:1

In the beginning God. . . .

Proverbs 6:6–11

Go to the ant, thou sluggard; consider her ways, and be wise: Which having no guide, overseer, or ruler, Provideth her meat in the summer, and gathereth her food in harvest. How long wilt thou sleep, O sluggard? when wilt thou arise out of thy sleep? Yet a little sleep, a little slumber, a little folding of the hands to sleep: So shall thy poverty come as one that travelleth, and thy want as an armed man.

Proverbs 10:4

He becometh poor that dealeth with a slack hand: but the hand of the diligent maketh rich.

Proverbs 20:22

[B]ut wait on the LORD, and he shall save thee.

Isaiah 40:31

But they that wait upon the LORD shall renew their strength; they shall mount up with wings as eagles; they shall run, and not be weary; and they shall walk, and not faint.

Jeremiah 6:16

Thus saith the LORD, Stand ye in the ways, and see, and ask for the old paths, where is the good way, and walk therein, and ye shall find rest for your souls. But they said, We will not walk therein.

Lamentations 3:25–26

The LORD is good unto them that wait for him, to the soul that seeketh him. It is good that a man should both hope and quietly wait for the salvation of the LORD.

Matthew 7:7–8

Ask, and it shall be given you; seek, and ye shall find; knock, and it shall be opened unto you: For every one that asketh receiveth; and he that seeketh findeth; and to him that knocketh it shall be opened.

Ephesians 2:8–9

For by grace are ye saved through faith; and that not of yourselves: it is the gift of God: Not of works, lest any man should boast.

Colossians 4:5

Walk in wisdom toward them that are without, redeeming the time.

Titus 3:14

And let ours also learn to maintain good works for necessary uses, that they be not unfruitful.

James 1:22

But be ye doers of the word, and not hearers only, deceiving your own selves.

James 2:17

Even so faith, if it hath not works, is dead, being alone.

Choose to Negate Negative Thinking

Proverbs 23:7

For as he thinketh in his heart, so is he. . . .

Isaiah 26:3

Thou wilt keep him in perfect peace, whose mind is stayed on thee: because he trusteth in thee.

Romans 8:6

For to be carnally minded is death; but to be spiritually minded is life and peace.

Romans 12:2

And be not conformed to this world: but be ye transformed by the renewing of your mind, that ye may prove what is that good, and acceptable, and perfect, will of God.

2 Corinthians 10:3–5

For though we walk in the flesh, we do not war after the flesh: (For the weapons of our warfare are not carnal, but mighty through God to the pulling down of strong holds;) Casting down imaginations, and every high thing that exalteth itself against the knowledge of God, and bringing into captivity every thought to the obedience of Christ . . .

Philippians 2:5

Let this mind be in you, which was also in Christ Jesus . . .

Philippians 4:8

Finally, brethren, whatsoever things are true, whatsoever things are honest, whatsoever things are just, whatsoever things are pure, whatsoever things are lovely, whatsoever things are of good report; if there be any virtue, and if there be any praise, think on these things.

Philippians 4:11

I have learned, in whatsoever state I am, therewith to be content.

Choose to Give of Yourself to Others, Allowing Others to Give to You, in a Manner That Is Constructive

Proverbs 11:25

The liberal soul shall be made fat: and he that watereth shall be watered also himself.

Proverbs 22:9

He that hath a bountiful eye shall be blessed; for he giveth of his bread to the poor.

Proverbs 28:27

He that giveth unto the poor shall not lack: but he that hideth his eyes shall have many a curse.

Ecclesiastes 4:9–10

Two are better than one; because they have a good reward for their labour. For if they fall, the one will lift up his fellow. . . .

Matthew 6:1

Take heed that ye do not your alms before men, to be seen of them: otherwise ye have no reward of your Father which is in heaven.

Luke 6:38

Give, and it shall be given unto you; good measure, pressed down, and shaken together, and running over, shall men give into your bosom. For with the same measure that ye mete withal it shall be measured to you again.

John 3:16

For God so loved the world, that he gave his only begotten Son, that whosoever believeth in him should not perish, but have everlasting life.

Acts 20:35

I have shewed you all things, how that so labouring ye ought to support the weak, and to remember the words of the Lord Jesus, how he said, It is more blessed to give than to receive.

1 Corinthians 10:31

[W]hatsoever ye do, do all to the glory of God.

2 Corinthians 9:6–7

But this I say, He which soweth sparingly shall reap also sparingly; and he which soweth bountifully shall reap also bountifully. Every man according as he purposeth in his heart, so let him give; not grudgingly, or of necessity: for God loveth a cheerful giver.

Galatians 6:7

Be not deceived; God is not mocked: for whatsoever a man soweth, that shall he also reap.

Galatians 6:10

As we have therefore opportunity, let us do good unto all men, especially unto them who are of the household of faith.

Philippians 2:4

Look not every man on his own things, but every man also on the things of others.

APPENDIX B

The ABCs of Being "In Him"

These are words spoken by the great master teacher, Jesus Christ, to his disciples:

> These things I have spoken unto you, that **in me** ye might have peace. In the world ye shall have tribulation: but be of good cheer; I have overcome the world. (John 16:33— Emphasis added)

Accordingly, tribulation/stress is part of the human condition and cannot be entirely avoided. Indeed, to do so would render one lifeless. However, we are also told that we are not destined to become hopeless victims of its potentially dangerous and deleterious effects. Rather, there is provision for us to *overcome* such challenges, maintaining a state of psychological equilibrium that Saint Paul subsequently described as transcending human understanding. The key to entering and remaining in this most desirable state is being *In Him* as follows:

> But whoso keepeth his word, in him verily is the love of God perfected: hereby know we that we are **in him.** (1 John 2:5—Emphasis added)

The Holy Scriptures reveal to us that the *Word* was *in the beginning*, that it *was with God*, and that it *was God* (John 1:1). We are also told that in Jesus *the Word was made flesh, and dwelt among us* (John 1:14).

I am asking you to be careful what you do with Jesus. As a Christian, I believe this choice will determine your eternal destiny. Consequently, it is the most important decision you will ever make. Accordingly, I invite you to ask Him to establish His kingdom within your heart, if you have not done so previously. Accepting His invitation to come into your heart, believing He died to pay for your sins, and confessing you have sinned and desire His forgiveness will establish this divine relationship according to His Word.

ACCEPT

Behold, I stand at the door, and knock: if any man hear my voice, and **open** the door, I will come in to him, and will sup with him, and he with me. (Revelation 3:20—Emphasis added)

BELIEVE

For God so loved the world, that he gave his only begotten Son, that whosoever **believeth** in him should not perish, but have everlasting life. (John 3:16—Emphasis added)

CONFESS

If we **confess** our sins, he is faithful and just to forgive us our sins, and to cleanse us from all unrighteousness. (1 John 1:9—Emphasis added)

ABIDE

I am the vine, ye are the branches: He that abideth in me, and I in him, the same bringeth forth much fruit: for without me ye can do nothing. . . . If ye keep my commandments, ye shall **abide** in my love; even as I have kept my Father's commandments, and abide in his love. (John 15:5 & 10— Emphasis added)

APPENDIX C

A Response to His Invitation

Lord Jesus, I choose to accept your invitation to dwell within my heart. I believe that God the Father sent you, his son, to earth to die for my sins. I confess all of my sins and ask for your forgiveness. Thank you for dying for my redemption. I will strive to abide in you, allowing your divine Word to abide in me. I recognize that in you I am a child of the God of love and that it gives him great pleasure to give to me his spirit of peace. You are my refuge; I will always trust in you. It is in your name that I offer my prayer. Amen.

According to Ephesians 2:8–9, our salvation is *the gift of God* that is made available to us *through faith* and *by grace*. Salvation is a word used to describe how we are resurrected spiritually from death in our sins to eternal life in Jesus Christ. Thus, we are *born again*. I especially like the manner in which my pastor describes the nature of the grace involved in the presentation of this miraculous gift:

- Judgment is getting what I deserve.

- Mercy is not getting what I deserve.

- Grace is getting what I do not deserve.

If you just prayed to accept Jesus Christ as Lord and Savior for the first time, or if yours was a recommitment, I encourage you to share your good news with someone who has matured in their Christian experience. Allow that person to mentor you as you continue to develop in your relationship with God. Although I am more interested in your relationship with God than with your religion, I also encourage you to become involved in a Bible-centered church that emphasizes Christian growth, service, and accountability. Feed your mind and spirit by reading, studying, and meditating upon the scriptures. Read other books that encourage your faith. My recommendations include *The Case for Christ* and *The Case for Faith* by the *New York Times* best-selling author Lee Strobel.

In Christ you are now *a new creature* (2 Corinthians 5:17). However, God's kingdom has an *adversary* known as *the devil*, who is described *as a roaring lion* whose mission is to *devour* us (1 Peter 5:8). But you have assurance when you are in Him that *greater is he that is in you, than he that is in the world* (1 John 4:4).

While we are instructed not to sin, it is recognized that in this life we are not yet perfected. So we are instructed that *if any man sin, we have an advocate with the Father, Jesus Christ* (1 John 2:1). Accordingly, it follows that *he is the propitiation for our sins: and not for ours only, but also for the sins of the whole world* (1 John 2:2). So when like the rest of us, you do make a mistake, pray and ask God for forgiveness in the name of your new advocate, Jesus. Celebrate God's grace and look forward to experiencing a whole life in the midst of a broken world!

Sources/References

Achor, Shawn. 2010. *The Happiness Advantage.* New York: Crown Business.

Adams, Bob. 2001. *The Everything Time Management Book.* Holbrook, MA: Adams Media Corp.

Albrecht, Karl. 1979. *Stress and the Manager.* New York: Simon & Schuster.

Allen, James. 1985. *As A Man Thinketh.* Fort Worth, TX: Brownlow.

Bandura, Albert. 1997. *Self-efficacy: The Exercise of Control.* New York: Freeman.

_____. 1977. "Self-efficacy: Toward a Unifying Theory of Behavioral Change." *Psychological Review* 84: 191–215.

Benson, Herbert, and William Proctor. 1984. *Beyond the Relaxation Response.* New York: Times Books.

_____, and Miriam Z. Klipper. 2008. *The Relaxation Response.* New York: William Morrow.

Burka, Jane B., and Lenora M. Yuen. 2008. *Procrastination: Why You Do It, What to Do About It Now.* Cambridge, MA: Da Capo Press.

Butler-Bowdon, Tom. 2007. *50 Psychology Classics.* Boston: Nicholas Brealey.

Charlesworth, Edward A., and Ronald G. Nathan. 1985. *Stress Management: A Comprehensive Guide To Wellness*. rev. ed. New York: Ballantine Books.

Colbert, Don. 2005. *Stress Less*. Lake Mary, FL: Siloam.

Covey, Stephen R. 1990. *The Seven Habits of Highly Effective People*. New York: Simon & Schuster.

_____, A. Roger Merrill, and Rebecca R. Merrill. 1995. *First Things First*. New York: Simon & Schuster.

de Posada, Joachim, and Ellen Singer. 2005. *Don't Eat the Marshmallow . . . Yet!* New York: Penguin.

Douthat, Ross. 2012. *Bad Religion*. New York: Free Press.

D'Souza, Dinesh. 2008. *What's So Great about Christianity*. Carol Stream, IL: Tyndale House.

Duhigg, Charles. 2012. *The Power of Habit*. New York: Random House.

Ellis, Albert, and Robert A. Harper. 1975. *A New Guide to Rational Living*. North Hollywood, CA: Wilshire Book Company.

Follette, John. 2010. *Broken Bread*. Grand Rapids, MI: Christian Classics Ethereal Library. e-book.

Frankl, Victor. 1963. *Man's Search for Meaning*. New York: Washington Square.

Frost, Robert. 1969. "The Road Not Taken." In *The Poetry of Robert Frost*, edited by Edward Connery Lathem. New York: Holt, Rinehart and Winston.

Gallwey, W. Timothy, Edward S. Hanzelik, and John Horton. 2009. *The Inner Game of Stress*. New York: Random House.

Glasser, William. 1999. *Choice Theory*. New York: Harper Perennial.

————. 2001. *Counseling with Choice Theory*. New York: HarperCollins.

————. 1975. *Reality Therapy*. New York: Harper and Row.

Goleman, Daniel. 1995. *Emotional Intelligence*. New York: Bantam.

Hanson, Peter G. 1986. *The Joy of Stress*. Kansas City, MO: Andrews and McMeel.

Harris, Gail. 1999. *Body & Soul*. New York: Kensington.

Herrin, Lisa Q. 2005. *Life Interrupted*. Chattanooga, TN: Living Ink Books.

Hiroto, Donald. 1974. "Locus of control and learned helplessness." *Journal of Experimental Psychology* 102: 187–93.

Iyengar, Sheena. 2010. *The Art of Choosing*. New York: Twelve.

Jones, Laurie Beth. 2004. *Jesus, Life Coach*. Nashville, TN: Thomas Nelson.

Kilpatrick, William K. 1993. *Why Johnny Can't Tell Right from Wrong*. New York: Touchstone.

Kubler-Ross, Elisabeth. 1969. *On Death and Dying*. New York: Macmillan.

_____, and David Kessler. 2007. *On Grief and Grieving*. paperback ed. New York: Scribner.

Landau, Meryl Davids. 2012. "Going Haywire." In *Best Hospitals. U. S. News & World Report*.

Losada, Marcial, and E. Heaphy. 2004. "The role of positivity and connectivity in the performance of business teams: A nonlinear dynamics model." *American Behavioral Scientist* 47 (6): 740–65.

Lucado, Max. 2007. *3:16*. Nashville, TN: Thomas Nelson.

Lyubomirsky, S., L. King, and E. Diener. 2005. "The benefits of frequent positive affect: Does happiness lead to success?" *Psychological Bulletin* 131: 803–55.

Maxwell, John C. 2011. *Beyond Talent*. Nashville, TN: Thomas Nelson.

_____. 2009. *How Successful People Think*. New York: Center Street.

McCain, John, with Mark Salter. 2007. *Character Is Destiny*. New York: Random House.

McClellan, Stephanie, Beth Hamilton, and Diane Reverand. 2010. *So Stressed*. New York: Free Press.

McMillan, Beverly. 2006. *Human Body*. Buffalo, NY: Firefly Books.

Miller, Lyle H., Alma Dell Smith, and Larry Rothstein. 1993. *The Stress Solution*. New York: Pocket Books.

Minirth, Frank. 2004. *Choosing Happiness Even When Life Is Hard*. Grand Rapids, MI: Fleming H. Revell.

————, and Paul Meier. 2002. *Happiness Is a Choice*. Grand Rapids, MI: Fleming H. Revell.

Nee, Watchman. 1997. *The Overcoming Life*. Anaheim, CA: Living Stream Ministry.

Newberry, Tommy. 2007. *The 4:8 Principle*. Carol Stream, IL: Tyndale House.

Pajares, Frank. 1996. "Self-efficacy beliefs in academic settings." *Review of Educational Research* 66: 543–78.

Pink, Daniel H. 2005. *A Whole New Mind*. New York: Penguin Group.

Peale, Norman V. 1978. *The Power of Positive Thinking*. Pawling, NY: Foundation for Christian Living.

Peterson, C., and L. C. Barrett. 1987. "Explanatory style and academic performance among university freshmen." *Journal of Personality and Social Psychology* 53: 603–07.

Post, Stephen, and Jill Neimark. 2007. *Why Good Things Happen to Good People*. New York: Broadway Books.

Powell, John. 1978. *Unconditional Love*. Allen, TX: Argus Communications.

Rodin, Judith, and Ellen Langer. 1977. "Long-term effects of a control-relevant intervention with the institutionalized aged." *Journal of Personality and Social Psychology* 35 (12): 897–902.

Rogers, George L., ed. 1996. *Benjamin Franklin's The Art of Virtue*. Midvale, UT: Choice Skills.

Sapolsky, Robert M. 2010. *Stress and Your Body*. Chantilly, VA: The Teaching Company.

_____. 2004. *Why Zebras Don't Get Ulcers*. 3rd ed. New York: Henry Holt, 2004.

Schweikart, Larry, and Michael Allen. 2004. *A Patriot's History of the United States*. New York: Penguin Group.

Seligman, Martin. 2002. *Authentic Happiness*. New York: Free Press.

_____. 2011. *Flourish*. New York: Free Press.

_____. 1998. *Learned Optimism*. 2nd ed. New York: Free Press.

Selye, Hans. 1975. *Stress Without Distress*. New York: NAL Penguin.

_____. 1984. *The Stress of Life*. rev. ed. New York: McGraw Hill.

Steel, Piers. 2011. *The Procrastination Equation*. New York: HarperCollins.

Stoop, David. 1982. *Self-Talk: Key to Personal Growth*. Old Tappan, NJ: Fleming H. Revell.

_____. 2006. *You Are What You Think*. Grand Rapids, MI: Fleming H. Revell.

Strobel, Lee. 1998. *The Case for Christ*. Grand Rapids, MI: Zondervan.

_____. 2000. *The Case for Faith*. Grand Rapids, MI: Zondervan.

Swindoll, Charles R. 1981. *Improving Your Serve: The Art of Unselfish Living*. Waco, TX: Word.

Talbott, Shawn. 2007. *The Cortisol Connection*. Alameda, CA: Hunter House.

Tedeschi, R. G., L. G. Calhoun, and A. Cann. 2007. "Evaluating resource gain: Understanding and misunderstanding posttraumatic growth." *Applied Psychology: An International Review* 56 (3): 396–406.

Toffler, Alvin. 1971. *Future Shock*. New York: Bantam Books.

Turley, Robert J. 1998. *The Choices Are Yours*. Highland City, FL: Rainbow Books.

Walker, Paul L. 1978. *Courage for Crisis Living.* Old Tappan, NJ: Fleming H. Revell.

Warren, Kay. 2012. *Choose Joy.* Grand Rapids, MI: Fleming H. Revell.

Warren, Rick. 2002. *The Purpose-Driven Life.* Grand Rapids, MI: Zondervan.

White, E. B. 1952. *Charlotte's Web.* New York: Harper & Brothers.

About the Author

The COPING Strategy was birthed decades ago as a product of Larry Gillespie's academic studies, on-the-job experience as a school psychologist, and Judeo-Christian heritage. After he incorporated this strategy into his own practice, its utility drew the attention of a number of his colleagues, who found it most helpful in their own practices. Professionals and non-professionals alike began to encourage Larry to share this phenomenal strategy with others in a format that has proven as easy to apply as it is powerful for change across cultures and creeds.

Currently, Larry and his wife Diane spend much of their time sharing the COPING Strategy with individuals and groups through printed and electronic formats and training activities. Knowing this strategy reveals their shared vision and mission. Consistently applying this strategy empowers individuals to share their experience of choosing a life of wholeness in a broken world.

Gillespie is a retired school psychologist; he resides in North Florida with his wife Diane, who is a registered nurse. He attended the University of North Florida, where he completed his undergraduate work in education and psychology, earned a master's degree in counseling, and completed additional graduate work in school psychology.